A FISHERMAN'S FORTUNE

A Memoir

Roger Jones

Print ISBN 9781838075248

Published by
Llyfrau Cambria Books, Wales, United Kingdom.
*Cambria Books is an imprint of
Cambria Publishing Ltd.*
Discover our other books at: www.cambriabooks.co.uk

CONTENTS

Preface

Life is not a straight line. Neither is it a neat arc. It is a scribble of lines that seem to be headed firmly to satisfying ends but sometimes double back on themselves, overlap or even sometimes appear to vanish completely.

When in latter age we think about our life there is a compulsion to see how and why certain events took place, or were even ordained, seemingly. Especially when one sits down to write down one's life story, there is a strong motivation to see the narrative shape of it all. The most obvious narrative shape of course is to follow chronology. This happened and then this other thing happened. But, as E. M Forster once pointed out, there is a big difference between 'The king died and then the queen died' and 'The king died *because* the queen died.' I think it is more interesting to question the causality of one's life than merely list events.

I have decided in this memoir to follow a rough chronological path, from childhood through to university days and then into industry and ultimately into public service. But it does not tell the whole story. Where do my social life and my family life fit in? I was not always too busy for any recreation, although I was invariably industrious, I admit. How do I give a picture of my attitudes, views and opinions if I merely detail the positions I held, the deals I struck, the business decisions I made?

When someone asks you, 'Who are you?' you can respond in a number of ways. Most people say, 'I am a postman', 'I am a teacher', 'I am a telesales operative', or whatever. It is a natural instinct to explain who you are in terms of your working life. I find it harder to define myself in this fashion. True, I am a pharmacist; it is the profession I trained for. I am more than that, even in terms of my working life, however. I regard myself as a curious soul, and therefore I am a scientist and researcher as much as simply a pharmacist. As will become abundantly clear, I am also a businessman. I would expand that term though; I am an entrepreneur. But these roles still do not define me. I have been, and still am to a certain extent, a public servant. I have tried, and continue to try, to influence policy and facilitate delivery across a range of aspects of public life. I will document these more fully in Chapter 6. I am a member of a prestigious London club and founder member of a learned society. I am a knight of the realm, though I do not often use my title, as can be seen from the title page of this memoir. But I am also a son, a brother, a father, a husband and a grandfather. I am a Welshman, and that aspect of my identity is very important to me. I am also a fisherman.

In writing this book I have become increasingly aware that there are themes and motifs that recur in one's life. I will begin my narrative by saying something of my early life and the passion for fishing that I shared with my father. I will conclude this personal account of my life with a chapter on fishing, but the business of trying to battle with and outwit one's opponent, aquatic or otherwise, is a strong thread that runs throughout this narrative. There are other recurrent strands too. I love motor cars and I love trains, as will become evident. I am an avid reader and I love to solve crossword puzzles. I like to listen to a range of musical genres. International travel has played an important part in my life. More seriously, education will be a theme that I return to repeatedly. Almost above all, my national identity as a Welshman runs like a golden vein through the ore of the experiences I will recount here.

I will try to show how various events and personalities have helped me make sense of my scribbled existence. Accordingly, I will sometimes sacrifice chronological urges in an attempt to give a certain thematic shape to this story. Occasionally I may jump back in time to explain an occurrence or say something further about one of the characters in my story. I intend to leave a lot of detail about my domestic life till the latter part of the book, but that does not deny the significance of my family and friends in any way. They will readily understand that. I have received honours in the public world, but the greatest honour in my life has been to know and love such people.

Someone once said all fiction is autobiography and all autobiography is fiction. I have tried to be completely truthful in the following pages, but we all know memory can be faulty and no one much wants to portray themselves in a bad light. If I sound immodest, please forgive me. If my rage at the incompetence I have encountered in most of the fields in which I have engaged comes across as arrogance, please forgive that too.

Chapter 1 *Early Years*

If you introduce kids to fishing, they become good citizens

Rex Hunt

Nothing much of import happened in North Wales on July 2nd, 1943. Three months earlier Martin Bormann had been appointed Hitler's second-in-command as Sir Henry Wood, the Chancellor of the Exchequer, was pointing out in the House of Commons that the war with Germany had so far cost Britain £13 billion. An American actor, Charles Ludlam, was also born in New York on the same day as these events. He was to become famous for his outrageous dress style and his Ridiculous Theatre Company. But July 2nd was not budget day, and Hitler had promoted enough of his acolytes. There are no records of anybody particularly outrageous being born. It was mainly a day that was notable for the sinking of a U-boat in The Bay of Biscay and for the fact that a certain lieutenant Charles Hall became the first black US pilot to shoot down a Nazi plane.

This day was particularly momentous for me, however, because it was the day, a warm cloudless Monday, when I entered the world. Like Charles Ludlam, I would go on to form my own series of companies too, but I think it is fair to say they have been rather more serious enterprises. I may also, in later public life, have been responsible for shooting down a number of public figures, figuratively speaking of course. April that year was the warmest April on record. Despite the financial burden of the war, the outlook was sunny, you might say.

I do not believe in astrology, or lucky numbers, or any unscientific nonsense about your life chances being determined by

4

anything but your background and your own efforts. However, in undertaking a little quirky research for this memoir, I discovered that because my July 2nd birth date contains the numbers 2, 7, 1, 9, 4 and 3, the number of my 'life path' is 8. Apparently, this number represents experience, authority and endeavour. I am, as a result, according to the folk who believe this sort of thing, gifted with natural leadership and the capacity to accumulate great wealth. I still think what wealth I have accrued is the reward of my own efforts though. And as for leadership, well, let others be the judge, I say. As a little addendum, I might add that the designated flower for my birth date is the larkspur, which represents haughtiness. Utter nonsense!

I was born in Denbigh Hospital and brought up in a little village called Carrog, in what was once the county of Merionethshire, but which now lies within the boundaries of Denbighshire. My mother Gwladys won a scholarship to Bangor Normal college to train as a schoolteacher and she taught for a number of years in a small village primary school in Gwyddelwern, where we lived when I was four years old. I suppose, looking back now, she just wanted to be safe, comfortable and normal. She lacked the ambition that my father always showed, and she was quite risk averse. An example of this was her insistence that my brother should become a teacher, because it was the safe option, with a good pension and so forth. I, on the other hand, was more of a wild child and immune from such safety-seeking urges.

My father was very different from my mother. He was a determined soul and money was a motivator. It was not that he wanted money for the prestige it might bring him in our small village, but more that he feared failure. Neither of my parents were particularly narrow minded, which perhaps would be a stereotype for members of a chapel-going small Welsh village community in the middle of the last century. But my parents had not experienced a great deal of the world, apart from a sojourn in London.

As stated, I was born on 2nd July, 1943 in Denbigh. My parents had just come back from London, where my father had worked in Harrods as a financial officer. They were anxious, of course, to get away from the bombing of the city at that time. He had left school at

5

fourteen, because that was the only option in those days. His father had been killed in an accident at the quarry where he worked. Now as a breadwinner he went to work on the docks in Liverpool. It was a very precarious living because of the practice of dock workers being selected for work on a daily basis. I recall seeing *On the Waterfront* with Marlon Brando as an American, and, I may say, slightly more glamorous, counterpart and it was this view of the hardships of such work that helped me to understand more fully my father's subsequent fervour to better his life and provide a good living for us as a family.

There was a good deal of nepotism and favouritism involved in the selection processes at the docks and my father was lucky to get more than a couple of days' work a week. This was not even enough to cover the cost of his digs, but he was fortunate, in one regard, in that he had two brothers, who were both schoolteachers, and they supported him during these trying times. Nevertheless, life could not have proceeded in this manner for very long. So, his mother, my grandmother, took it upon herself to intervene. She had been in service in Sloane Square in London from the age of thirteen and therefore knew people who had important connections. Desperate circumstances call for desperate measures, so she wrote to her former employers to see if they could help my father. They in turn got in touch with London's top department store and he was offered a job working in Harrod's bank. It was a very junior position, of course, but he was a bright man who was astute enough to catch out several frauds within the bank and consequently he quickly rose to the more senior position of chief cashier.

He had been born in Corris, near Machynlleth, and he was christened Richard. His great love was fishing, and he taught me all I know about the sport. Whenever people ask me what it is that makes someone a great fisherman, I always tell them it is knowledge of the water. You get a feeling that a certain spot would be a place that fish would like. In a way it is achieving an understanding of the psychology of your prey that makes you a good fisherman. From what I have read and from what I have heard from scientists who are fellow fishing enthusiasts, salmon can probably extract energy from the stream where they come to spawn. They will set themselves in a certain geostatic position and allow the current of water to cross their back and create kinetic electrical energy, which is transformed to chemical energy and thence to physical energy. Salmon, of course, do not eat anything in fresh water. They will have spent three years in the sea but when they enter fresh water they are merely curious about the things they see. The fisherman's hook is just an object to them, not necessarily a danger. It is remarkable that their sense of smell allows them to locate the exact place where they were spawned. Of course, salmon are not the only creatures that feel compelled to return to their homeland, having spent a good portion of their lives in the great oceans, or great cities, as was the case for me, and I suspect, a number of my Welsh countrymen.

I have few memories of my very earliest years, but one thing stands out clearly. It dates from 1947 when for some reason I was looking out of the window awaiting my father's return home and I saw him trudging towards our house carrying his bicycle over his shoulders. It was a remarkable sight. It was not, as you might expect, a result of a puncture but because of the heavy snow that had prevented him riding home. It was a strange apparition to me, though I could not realise, because I was only four years old, that here was a metaphor for his current situation in life, at least if the bicycle were a symbol of the economic burden he had to bear.

I also have fond memories of our pet, a little terrier called Pwtin, which derives from the Welsh word *pwt*, meaning small, with the diminutive 'in' added, to emphasize how small, I suppose. The name is not, I would hasten to add, to be confused with the name Putin or another word suggesting ill repute, the French *putain*.

I am sorry to say I do not have such memories of my extended family. On my father's side I have two uncles and an aunt. My uncles were both teachers and their sister was a housewife, or homemaker, as is now the preferred term. I have cousins, but I saw little of them when I was growing up.

I have an elder brother, who, like my mother and uncles, became a teacher. We were very unalike. When my mother died at the ripe old age of a hundred and one, he claimed that he should inherit the family home. He said that my mother preferred him to me, but that was nonsense. The point was that the will was very badly constructed. My mother knew that and wanted me to become an executor, but my brother used his daughter's common law husband, a lawyer, to point out that there was a lot of ambiguity and confusion in the wording of the document. I would go as far as to say it was a badly written will, drawn up by a knave. The house that he acquired was a big house, in fact not just a dwelling, but also the local post office, which my mother had taken over when she gave up her teaching job to become a postmistress.

Carrog is a small village of about five hundred souls, all of the native dwellers Welsh-speaking of course, though as time went by there was an influx of English families from Cheshire and Lancashire seeking to retire to the calmer waters of North Wales. It might surprise some readers, but there was hardly any antipathy towards these invaders, or newcomers. Everybody tries to integrate as best they can, I suppose. My mother was a leading light in the Women's Institute in this small but close community. My father had the job he had wanted all his life – a badly supervised position which gave him the freedom to pursue his love of fishing. He was what you might call sharp. Not a rogue, but not a man to miss an opportunity. He had aspirations to be a businessman and make as much money as possible, but his job with the council gave him too much leisure time (when he could go fishing) to embark upon a business venture of his own. Accordingly, he persuaded my mother to leave the teaching profession for the retail and post office trade, though she was not entirely happy about this decision. Both my parents were in their early forties at this time.

The first home I have any vivid memories of was a council house - 4 Maes y Llan – in Carrog. When we came to Carrog in 1947 it was the time of the great floods caused by the snow melt of the horrific winter of 1947. I was only four years old, but I have a thrilling memory of seeing whole trees floating down the river Dee, which had burst its banks. At this time we lived in the Methodist chapel house - 'Disgwylfa'. My mother had been providing the Minister, a man called Evan Lynch, with food, so she was his

8

housekeeper in all but name. The whole family was allowed to move into the chapel house, or manse, while we were applying for a council house. I suspect my father's connections in the council offices were helpful in our obtaining a suitable house. My father was not going to settle for a modest council house, however; he wanted something more substantial.

He saw the local post office come onto the market in 1951. He had the very natural desire to be a homeowner, rather than a council tenant, so he raised enough money to purchase our new home, and the business that went with it. He had also acquired a car, which was something of a rarity in those far off days. It was a Wolseley Hornet, with the licence plate JR 2440. Since his name was Richard Jones, the letters provided a sort of inverted personalised numberplate. I do not know if there was any vanity involved here or whether it was just a coincidence, but perhaps it was a sort of statement, and perhaps I have inherited the gene for this, because I do have a personalised numberplate myself. It cost considerably more, I might add. My present numberplate is 5RJ, the number 5 standing in for the letter S of my title, Sir Roger Jones.

This plate was bought for me at auction by my wife. She went to the auction alone because I could not attend, for some reason. She intended to bid for a particular plate - RSJ 1 - but there was someone bidding against her and the price rocketed, so she let it go to the other bidder, a car dealer from Reading. He told her,' It's no good you ringing me up after the auction because I have no intention of selling it.' My wife said, 'I didn't think you wanted to buy it on order to sell it again. I would have thought you'd be buying it in order to enjoy it.' Later on in the auction 5RJ came up, which in her opinion was a far better numberplate. The auctioneer announced to the assembled hopeful buyers, 'We all know what the blonde lady is prepared to pay, don't we?' Actually, what she paid was very reasonable. Then the car dealer from Reading began ringing us up trying to sell us the numberplate he had bought, knowing he had paid too much for it. My wife gave him short shrift. 'Why on earth do you want to sell something you obviously wanted so much,' she said to him. 'I'm so sorry, I thought you bought it to enjoy it.' Later, when she told me

9

about this, she concluded, 'Women 1, Men 0'.

My son is called Hefin and one day I saw there was a car in Machynlleth with the plate HEF 1N. Unfortunately, the owner was unwilling to sell it to me, despite my offer of £30,000, which I thought rather generous. There are not all that many people in Wales called Hefin, I suppose. Even fewer outside Wales, doubtless. So if it does come up for sale one day perhaps my son will get his own special personalised plate.

But back to the Wolseley. It was small but still regarded as a luxury marque in those days. One of my outstanding memories was being taken up to London in it when I was eight years old, to visit the Festival of Britain. Unlike the Great Exhibition held a century earlier, this display was designed to focus on purely British art, science, technology and design, rather than showpiece world or commonwealth innovations. The displays that interested me most concerned science and technology, and it may be the case that this prefigured my career choices a decade later. I was an avid reader and loved humanities and science subjects equally in secondary school but perhaps there was always a pull towards the sciences.

The house and post office we moved into was quite a substantial building. It had been built at a time when materials were reasonable cheap. Obviously, we were near the slate producing areas of Llanberis and Blaenau Ffestiniog, but the most important feature of our house was that it constructed using glazed brick. Bricks selected for glazing had to be very hard, so they were of the very highest quality. But in the glazing process sometimes bricks were chipped, and hence could not be used for decorative purposes, for instance as kitchen tiles. What builders did then was to turn them round and use them as ordinary bricks for wall construction.

There was only a small garden behind the post office but there was a field at the back of the house where local children played. This being the fifties, we played at war, and cowboys and Indians. We were always shooting each other, but fortunately, unlike in some countries, we grew out of that. We built dens; we read comics like *The Beano* and *The Dandy* and, when we wanted more excitement than Desperate Dan or Minnie the Minx could offer, *The Eagle*, which featured an even more desperate Dan, the space pilot Dan Dare. He engaged in a continual struggle to outwit The Mekon, a dome-headed futuristic villain. For those readers who are too young to remember these characters, Dan Dare was a sort of cartoon Tom Hanks hero and, if Hollywood made a live action film of this nonsense, I would suggest Dominic Cummings be cast as The Mekon.

I read books too, of course. Regular fare was Enid Blyton. I was guided by my mother to consume her entire oeuvre, I think. Some of my contemporaries were pointed towards H G Wells, Robert Louis Stevenson, R M Ballantyne, and other writers of classic boys' adventure yarns, but in my early years the choice, I fear, was *The Famous Five*, *The Secret Seven* or *The Barney Mysteries*. And *The Faraway Tree*, of course. People today are rather dismissive of Blyton's simplistic and repetitive output. Actually, Michael Rosen, who was Children's Laureate for a period in the first and second decades of this century, found himself 'flinching at the occasional outbursts of snobbery and the assumed level of privilege in the children and families presented in her books.' It is easy, looking back, to see that her world view was extremely limited, but I do not think I was aware of her snobbery, and I hope it did not influence me in any way. I tend to concur that the act of reading stories itself is a good thing, and Blyton certainly encouraged vast numbers of children to take up the reading habit.

In my teens I continued reading, and since I am bilingual, I read in Welsh as well as English. I enjoyed many of the adventure classics, like *Moby Dick*, *Treasure Island* and later, *Lord of the Flies*. In fact, I could have happily studied literature to a higher level, but I made a pragmatic decision to pursue the sciences because I viewed the job prospects in doing so as significantly more rewarding.

I also liked listening to the radio, particularly on a Sunday afternoon when *Beyond Our Ken* and *Round the Horne* were the comedy highlights of the week. These half hour programmes were sketch shows held together by a rather straightlaced establishment figure, Kenneth Horne, but included farcical and occasionally satirical moments of genius from people like Kenneth Williams, later

11

famous for his *Carry On* films, Ron Moody, who later played Fagin in *Oliver Twist*, Betty Marsden, Hugh Paddick and Bill Pertwee, who later exasperated everyone in his role of Warden Hodges in *Dad's Army*. These were simple times and I do not think I appreciated the double entendres and possibly homophobic references that abounded. I just found the catchphrases ('I'm Julian and this is my friend Sandy') and eccentric characters (Rambling Syd Rumpole, Fanny Haddock, Ricky Livid, Hankie Flowerd) hysterically funny. I do not think I even realised the outrageously camp Julian and Sandy and the spoof version of Frankie Howerd were clearly lampooning homosexuality.

I also loved *The Goon Show* and *Hancock's Half Hour*. These were unmissable programmes and in some ways I feel a little sad that younger people have never had the wonderful experience of hearing Tony Hancock's breathy, disconsolate, lugubrious voice introducing his show, and one's knowledge that yet again a little man with big pretensions was going to fail to impress those around him. And fail so amusingly, for we all enjoy a little schadenfreude, after all. The patent absurdity of the Goons was also very appealing to a teenager surrounded by so much seriousness. I was delighted by Peter Sellers as the diminutive and pathetic Bluebottle; by Spike Milligan as Eccles, a demented idiotic incompetent and by Harry Secombe as the hapless hero Neddy Seagoon. 'You dirty rotten scoundrel, you've deaded me,' Sellers would say in a squeaky little voice. It was simply funny that he was 'deaded' every week. And someone fell in the water every week, as Eccles would note cheerfully. These creations, and even the characters played by Ray Wellington, who could not appear in any modern show because of the obvious racist overtones, engendered a fan base that grew very quickly in the fifties. And I situated myself very firmly in that group.

I still listen to the radio, naturally. Radio Four is the channel I prefer, and that is nothing to do with the fact that I was a governor at the BBC for some years. I spent a lot of my working life travelling by car and accordingly l have listened to a lot of the output of this channel. As a result, actually, one of my roles at the BBC was as specialist governor for Radio Four.

The surrealist comedy of those Sunday afternoons and the serious and international new coverage of Radio Four were not to everyone's taste in my family. My grandmother, my father's mother, was a character, but she was not one for levity, and I am not sure she had a very wide appreciation of world events. She was a real matriarch and self-appointed guardian of the family's spiritual welfare. She was born in Victorian times and not to a family of privilege, so life was hard. When she was working as a maid for a family in Sloane Square she had a very restricted life, only being allowed a short spell outside the house on a Sunday afternoon. She would tell stories from her youth of the exploits of Jack the Ripper, but for the most part she was not a born entertainer. She was deeply religious, or perhaps it is truer to say she was very keen to appear so. She always had a Bible open on her knee, particularly when she knew she was expecting visitors whom she could impress with her devotion.

I am a believer myself, but not with the same fervour. She would have liked to inculcate her beliefs in me, but I fear we did not speak the same language. I am speaking figuratively here of course. She was obsessed by religious dogma, but I hated the endless sermons and droning hymns. On Sundays I had to attend chapel in the morning, go to Sunday School in the afternoon and then go to the evening service. I would have preferred to go fishing but I had to content myself with the radio or the occasional walk. Even then my grandmother was sceptical about me going out because she suspected my motivation was to find out where the fish were, not simply to ruminate on that morning's sermon.

I never knew my paternal grandfather, who was killed in an accident at the Graig Lelo stone quarry, but my grandmother's influence was considerable. She used to spend two months at a time with each of her four children, so she would be moving from family to family throughout the year and therefore twice a year she would descend on us, like a lone horsewoman of the apocalypse. Perhaps she thought she did so in order to help her sons' families, but in truth she did not do very much in a practical sense. She merely sat in our living room with her Bible on her knee.

I know my family did not possess a television set at the time of the coronation of Queen Elizabeth, but I believe we acquired one shortly after, a black and white Murphy 14", probably in a walnut case, I imagine. My grandmother had some arcane beliefs; one being that you should never leave a socket without a bulb, because the electricity would drip out. Another was that not only were we watching the newsreaders and presenters on the screen, but they were also watching us. An early conspiracy theorist, you might say. She would look at Chris Michealmore, which was the name she attributed to Cliff Michelmore, the longstanding BBC presenter, and ask him what he thought about her grandson, who had just walked into the room having returned home triumphantly with several fish hanging from his arm. Cliff Michelmore remained impassive, needless to say.

Food was quite different from the rich and varied options available today. All through the winter there would be a huge pot of what was called 'lobscouse' simmering away on the cooker. I would typically have a bowl of it when I came home for lunch from primary school, but my mother was continually adding to it, so it never seemed to run out. Lobscouse was a version of what many Welsh families would term *cawl*, or lamb stew, as it might be called in other parts of the country, but more often it was beef that was the meat constituent. Though North German in origin, it came to be a staple food in Liverpool, and it is believed that the term 'scouser' for Liverpudlians derives from this corruption of the German term *labskaus*.

In addition to this staple there would be a roast joint of meat on a Sunday but, perhaps surprisingly, very little fish was eaten in our house, despite my enthusiasm, and that of my father, for catching the blighters. And that is not a misprint of bloaters. We were, of course, a Methodist family and not constrained by the custom of eating fish on a Friday, as our Catholic neighbours might have been.

There was an obvious reason for our reluctance to eat our catch. Salmon could be readily sold to local restaurants and hotels, and they would fetch a pound per pound in weight. A typical well grown salmon might weigh in at ten pounds avoirdupois: this translated to ten pounds sterling, or a week's wages for a lot of people. And the local hotels were always only too ready to buy from my father and me. We also sold to wholesalers, who were happy to trade with us. I think my entrepreneurial instincts were not fully formed at this age, but they were evidently only waiting to be unearthed, as I hope to demonstrate in due course.

As far as food likes and dislikes are concerned, I loved rabbit pie. Up until the time of myxomatosis at least. This was a disease lethal to rabbits that decimated the rabbit population in Britain in the early fifties. Farmers naturally welcomed the fact that a serious and longstanding pest was being eliminated, but those who enjoyed rabbit pie deplored the loss of such a food source. My mother was a superb cook, however, though of course not an adventurous one. And I always ate very well.

On the other hand, I hated rice pudding. This was something that I was subjected to in my secondary school days, when I had school dinners. Rice, and its evil twin siblings tapioca and sago pudding, appeared too often for my liking, tormenting my teenager's healthy appetite. I could cope with prunes and custard, regarded as a healthy dessert in those days, but I also felt great antipathy towards mashed potato. Not necessarily because of the hard bullet-like lumps that would be lodged in the spoonful that you received from a surly dinner lady, more because it seemed just so much stodge to me.

In primary school I obviously enjoyed doing sums, as we termed Mathematics, but I hated doing Art because it seemed we were always compelled to work with stencils. I assume now I objected to the constraints that were being imposed upon me. And it may be that I was already showing signs of my desire to be more creative in my thinking. I enjoyed History and Geography, but as for Science, my later love, we were not given scope to do much of that until I went to secondary school. What we were offered was Nature Study, which was not something I felt I could really get my teeth into.

I had a good friend called Delwyn at primary school, but we rather lost touch as he did not pass the eleven plus exam. Obviously, we had different experiences in our new schools and thus it was difficult to maintain our close friendship. I was fortunate to discover

15

a number of new friends when I went to Bala Boys' Grammar School, however. I enjoyed our outdoor adventures and playing with Meccano, a construction toy and a sort of forerunner of today's Lego, but increasingly fishing took up my leisure time. I think it is safe to say when I was not fishing, I was thinking about fishing. At Bala I was quite athletic. I played football, though I did not break into the school team. I played for the House, as we had a house system. I believe most grammar schools at that time adopted this system, intended to encourage loyalty and team spirit but really just aping the structure in place at public schools. And it was not only this feature that was imitated, for the school hall in our 1851 building was said to be modelled on Jesus College, Oxford.

Despite such pretensions, I would say that Bala Boys' Grammar was possibly the worst grammar school in the country at that time. Results were terrible; in fact it was a cause of great celebration if any boy managed to pass one of the science subjects at 'O' level. Despite this, or perhaps because the teaching was so bad that pupils made huge efforts to succeed, a number of my contemporaries did very well in later life. I am, in fact, one of three knights of the realm to emerge from those unhallowed halls. One, a man by the name of Robin Williams, became a scientific adviser to the Welsh government. Unlike me, he excelled at Physics. I would go as far as to say he was a genius. He was certainly more adept at the subject than our Physics teacher, a man we called Boliog, which is Welsh for Big Belly. Boliog tried to solve problems on the board but, to his dismay, and our equal measure of dismay and amusement, consistently failed, so it was no real wonder that so many of his young charges also failed.

The other schoolfellow who was awarded a knighthood was Rees Davies, sadly departed now. Rees was a historian and academic, lecturing at UCL, going on to become Professor of History at University College of Wales, Aberystwyth and then Professor of Medieval History at Oxford University. He was knighted in 2005 for services to History.

It is sad to say but I consider my days at Bala Boys' Grammar were something of a waste of time. You might expect, despite the inadequacies of their pedagogical styles, that my teachers would have at least instilled a sort of academic rigor in us, but I am afraid it was not so. A number of the staff had come back from serving in the Second World War and they did have a wider experience than some of the other teachers, but for the most part these men were intellectual lightweights. There were some eccentric teachers, for instance an English teacher who would take the sixth formers to Stratford-Upon-Avon. These school trips were the stuff of legend. I do not know if an appreciation of the subtleties of Shakespearian language was high on their priorities, but the opportunities provided for the boys to engage in a range of sexual encounters with sixth form girls was seized upon with great relish. There was also a Chemistry teacher called Mr Owens, who was a Welsh speaker from Anglesey who was amusing as far as he had a great store of Welsh expressions which he used to share with us. One of the most memorable was *Cledd a min yw colli mam,* which translates as 'sharp is the sword that inflicts the pain of losing a mother.' These aphorisms had little to do with Chemistry, but eccentricity was a byword for the teaching profession sixty years ago.

The headmaster was a man called Mr Pugh, Harri Pugh, who was a little man. In many ways. He expressed his diminutive intellectual status by standing by doors listening to his teachers, and by administering the cane to malfeasant boys.

Nevertheless, I had some good times with friends. I did not really have a gang, and we did not define ourselves in terms of prevailing fashion or musical trends – teddy boys had made their appearance in Britain in the mid- fifties, but they had not penetrated the environs of Bala. We bonded, I suppose, on our journeys to and from school. It was an eighteen-mile train journey from Carrog to Bala, by steam train, for these were the days before diesel and a good while before Dr Beeching decimated local train lines. The trip involved a wait in Bala junction, because the train went on to Dolgellau and we had to take a branch line to Bala. I would get up at seven o' clock every morning, catch the train from my village at eight o' clock and get to school for nine o' clock. It was a long day. And it was not over when I got home again, for we had homework to complete every night. Nobody seemed to bother marking it, but I probably learned more from studying for my homework than I did during the lessons, watching Bolliog puzzling over a Physics problem or listening to the gnomic ramblings of Mr Owens as he eschewed Chemistry for Welsh folk wisdom.

But I do not want to give the impression that school life was a blend of incompetent teachers and jolly japes with schoolfellow friends. My journeys to and from school were sometimes plagued by a bully by the name of John Alsop. The carriages did not have a corridor, so at every station boys would get into their regular self-contained compartment. You could not just wander into a compartment reserved for lads from another village. This meant if there was someone who was hostile or threatening you had to face him every day. John Alsop bullied lots of boys, but he had a particular penchant for taking out on my person whatever personal griefs he was suffering. He would hit me in the face, completely unprovoked, and though I hit him back he became more violent. The last I heard of him he was working as a laboratory assistant in a dairy. I do not know how successful he was in this career, but I am pretty certain he did not win a Nobel prize.

You have to stand up to bullies. When I became a BBC governor the chairman was a renowned bully, an Irishman by the name of Sir Christopher Bland. He was partial to bullying everyone in committee meetings, but he bullied women especially. At my first board meeting I had to say to him: 'If you ever speak to me the way you spoke to so and so today, we'll be at war. I won't stand for it.' So he never bullied me personally. Perhaps my dealings with John Alsop prepared me for this encounter. I digress, however, and I will go into further detail about my time at the BBC in a later chapter.

At school I was awarded a number of prizes for being best in form and best in year. These tended to be books or book tokens. I did not make the mistake of flaunting my successes, however, because I thought it best not to make myself a target for the envy of others. It is difficult sometimes.

We had French lessons at the girls' equivalent of my grammar school, so I encountered girls at the age of fifteen. End of term

18

dances became part of life, but not at Bala. They were events held in a village hall in a small town called Corwen, three miles from Carrog. We mainly entertained ourselves with folk dancing and square dancing, rather than the new fashions of jive and rock 'n' roll. I was aware of Elvis Presley and Buddy Holly, of course, but I was not so enamoured of jazz. My listening tastes were rather eclectic and though modern jazz was in vogue I preferred pop music. I had a Dansette record player, as did a lot of people in the late fifties and early sixties. They were incredibly expensive when they were first marketed in 1952 but were slightly more affordable when mine was bought. As a guide, the model I possessed cost slightly more than a week's wages for a sixteen-year-old office worker with five 'O' levels. I have discovered that the actual price was eleven guineas, but I hesitate to use the term 'guineas' when we now live in an age where even 'shillings and pence' are arcane terms to most people. Having said that I should mention that the record label Pye used to market a series of long-playing records as Golden Guinea LPs. These were often 'trad' jazz records, but such music was beginning to be superseded by rock 'n' roll. To me it was all 'pop' and I enjoyed Elvis, Cliff Richard, Tommy Steele and Johnny Ray as much as Kenny Ball's Jazzmen's 'Midnight in Moscow' or Acker Bilk's mournful 'Stranger on the Shore'. Strangely, I was also enamoured of show music, and bought LPs of the soundtracks of *Oklahoma*, *South Pacific*, *Guys and Dolls* and so forth.

The question WHY? hit me early in my schooldays. I guess I had a natural curiosity. About anything. About simple everyday occurrences such as the reason that one fish took the fly, and another one did not. Perhaps the presentation was not right. But obviously I was curious about more metaphysical concerns too. I was always looking for rational, logical explanations for phenomena. I suppose my grandmother had tried to inculcate in me her surplus of faith and belief, as for her it was almost sacrilegious to ask the question WHY. But happily, she did not succeed in that enterprise.

As far as social attitudes are concerned, I think I was bang middle of the road. I laughed at characters like John Inman's camp shop assistant in *Are You Being Served?* without realising how terribly stereotyping it was of the gay community. Of course, we did not even use the term 'gay' because we were unaware of its present usage. Apparently gay men had appropriated the word as a less clinical term for homosexuality well before the sixties, but it was not anything like as current as it is now. There were a couple of lads in my form who doubtless were gay - statistically it would have been very unlikely if there had not been any – but they were not treated badly. Rather, they were simply regarded as *different*. My friends did not bother with them, and neither did I. I fear I may have felt that if I had been closer to them, I might have been regarded as guilty by association. It must sound shocking now, to use that term 'guilty', but these were uninformed times.

I am happy to say, however, that I was not at all racist. I lived in a small village, it is important to recall, and immigration from the West Indies and Pakistan and Bangladesh had not made any impact on our little world. My first deep encounter with people of a very different culture was when I worked in Nigeria.

I had had good advice at one point, and that was to refrain from criticising people for things that they could not help being. This applied to those workers I met who had different beliefs and customs, and to those of my expat co-workers who did display racist attitudes. I knew that they could not help themselves, because of their upbringing, and it was not part of my remit to judge or try to educate them. Also, ethnic background does not necessarily determine a person's character. I met Nigerians who were thoroughly unpleasant, and I worked with British colleagues who were mean or superior and of poor understanding and intellect. And it stood me in good stead, the realisation that one's colour has nothing to do with one's temperament.

You cannot change history, so it pays to have a degree of acceptance of how things are. But I deplored some of the conservative attitudes I came across, both in school and university and in my working life. I was radical in my youth and hated the Conservative party. Remember, this was the era of that pompous old grouse-shooting Harold MacMillan and the dreadful Alec Douglas-Home, who Harold Wison memorably called 'a scion of an effete establishment'. The man who would soon replace Douglas-Home as prime minister regarded him, as did most of the country, as totally unsuited to deal with the dawning new age of technology. It is an odd fact that Douglas-Home was the only prime minister in our history who occupied that high office as neither a member of the House of Commons nor of the House of Lords, admittedly only for a period of twenty days. The reason for this was that he had renounced his peerage and was awaiting a by-election in a nice, safe Scottish seat. I have tempered my early radicalism somewhat over the years admittedly. It seems I have adhered to the maxim 'If you are not a communist at the age of twenty you have no heart; but if you are still a communist at the age of thirty you have no brain.'

As a young man I was reasonably well informed about world events, such as the election of J F Kennedy, the first ventures into space, and, of course, the fiasco of The Suez War, because I read what was then called The Manchester Guardian. Our shop sold newspapers, so I had access to a range of titles, but I avoided some of the more invidious organs, like *The Daily Mail,* in favour of papers that offered more considered and more moderate views.

I chose sciences to study at 'A' level, though perhaps they were not my best subjects. for I could easily have pursued my other interests, for instance in history and literature. I chose to take Biology and Chemistry and Physics, though I came to realise that one needs a good deal of higher mathematical knowledge to study Physics more successfully than I managed. Also, let it be said, the ineffectual teaching of that subject conspired against me. I became aware that our school was vastly inferior, in terms of results, to Llanelli Grammar School, for example, where every student passed Physics. I passed all three subjects, gaining an 'A' grade in Chemistry, a 'B' in Biology, but only a 'C' in Physics. I had chosen these subjects because I had a desire to study for a career in medicine, but these grades were not sufficient for a place at medical school. Because it was deemed likely that I would not achieve the top grades in all three subjects I was advised to apply to university to study Pharmacy and I did so, gaining a place at The Welsh School of Pharmacy in Cardiff College of Advanced Technology in

Cathays. CATs, as such institutions were called, were set up in the mid-fifties, but by the middle of the next decade they grew exponentially and the Welsh College of advanced Technology became The Institute of Science and Technology, or UWIST. Nowadays the School of Pharmacy is located within Cardiff University. I did not feel that I was in a less prestigious institution, despite my alma mater not having university status, because I was rather more concerned that I was on a three-year course, rather than the six-year course I would have had to pursue as a medical student. That was all that mattered to me, anxious as I was to get into the world and earn money, buy a car and so forth. I knew that I would not be in a position where I was earning less money than I would be as a doctor, and this choice of course meant that I stood to start earning that much sooner.

My degree was unclassified because it was a certificate rather than a full degree course. Then it was announced to me that the course, set by The Pharmaceutical Society, was going to discontinued entirely. In my cohort there were only five students and the lecturers asked us if we would be prepared to come back after the summer and sit an exam in the September. This would entitle us to a Bachelor of Pharmacy degree. I said they could count me in and thereby I got a degree without having to do another year's study. It was right and fair that they should do that, but of the five of us approached to sit the examination, only three passed. After graduating one had to do a year's apprenticeship in pharmacy to get your MPS, as it was known in those days. MPS stands for Membership of the Pharmaceutical Society, a qualification that enables you to dispense prescriptions, and other fine things. I went to work for Boots in Ruthin, in North Wales, in the first instance.

This year turned out to be a dreadful experience because I found myself being treated as little more than a shop assistant, filling shelves with dogfood and completing other such menial tasks. I was regarded as cheap labour; it might have been good for discipline, but it was bad for the soul. Working for Boots there was the opportunity to go on training courses at company headquarters in Nottingham, where Jesse Boot had first set up his 'chemist to the nation' retail business, born out of his father's modest herbalist shop, but I could not see myself progressing in the company. Instead, I decided to undertake some further study.

Accordingly, I applied to Bradford University to take a Masters degree in Finance and Economics. With that ticket, as I like to think of it, I knew I would be able to start earning some decent money. It was a wise choice, because Harold Wilson's government was stressing that the 'white heat of technology' was upon the country and people were waking up to a different world. I realised that there were thousands of young people leaving school and getting pharmacy degrees, but none of them could master a balance sheet. I knew I could afford to pay for the course because I was prepared to work weekends and evenings as a locum in various pharmacies. Then, of course, armed with a B.Pharm and a M.Sc. I was red meat for a range of pharmaceutical companies.

I have few regrets about this period of my life, but I have to say I would have loved to have studied medicine. I ended up with a fabulous job in Nigeria, but I was very envious of the medics I met. They were earning no more money than me, but they were certainly doing more good. There was a fork in the road, as there is for most people, and my exam results led me to take one avenue. I think now I made decisions which were right for me, and subsequently for my family.

I remember leaving for Cardiff as the first and only member of my family to go to university, as the CAT I attended was to become. My mother and brother both were professionals, but they went to teacher training college, and did not automatically obtain degrees. There was not much drama about my leaving the family home, however. My father and I did celebrate my return at the end of term over a pint in the local hostelry, not that he was much of a drinker. We started to talk man to man, rather than father to son, and I appreciated that I was experiencing an important rite of passage. Of course, I was already tied to my father with wires of steel through our mutual love of fishing, as I now realise.

Chapter 2 *University and After*

I didn't think I had time for fishing before I fished

Bob Mortimer

When I moved to Cardiff, I found digs in Macintosh Place. The following year I had digs in Howard Gardens and during my third year I lived in Canton.

It was certainly daunting going away for the first time in my life. When I joined the Welsh Pharmaceutical Students Association, I used to look at the club officers and regard them as objects of worship. I could never do what they were doing, I thought. They were only two or three years older than me, of course, but they seemed so much more knowledgeable and empowered. Their ease and eloquence made me vow to myself very early on that I would make every effort to become the President of the Welsh Pharmaceutical Students Association. I am happy to record that I succeeded in achieving this ambition.

As it was an elected role, I realised I would have to garner a certain popularity to be successful. I suppose I was affable enough, but I thought there might be certain strategies I might employ to increase my chances of gaining this important position. I played a lot of football, but I would often be happy to be substituted. Sometimes I would chalk myself up as a second half substitute, ensuring other people got game time; hence I never felt I was actively antagonising other players. Also, it was crucial to gain support from the female students. I do not wish to sound immodest, but I managed to get a sizeable number of those votes.

A fair number of young women would spend Friday nights at

the *Aelwyd*, the home of the *Urdd Gobaith Cymru* or Welsh Youth Organisation. The *Urdd,* as it is commonly known, translates as The League of Hope (for Wales). Meetings were held in the vestry of the chapel in Crwys Road in Cardiff. This building is now a Hindu temple. I was glad to meet girls there from other university departments than my own Pharmacy department. Also, there were girls not at university, but who worked for the BBC in Cardiff, for instance. I dated some of these young ladies, some only for a brief period, but I did see one girl for what seemed at the time quite a long while. I think it was for about a term, in point of fact. She was actually not someone I had met at Aelwyd, but a diminutive student from Ferzackerly in Liverpool, who was doing a technical course, as I recall. I was not very serious about relationships as a young man, I have to admit. Perhaps the amorous advances of the girls who worked on the counter while I was employed by Boots led me to think that being a pharmacist would never cause any great difficulties in this arena.

It was when I finished at the School of Pharmacy that I went to work at Boots in Ruthin. I did not have any great expectations of this work and I was therefore not too disappointed by the experience. It was during this time that I sustained the first of my driving accidents. I am almost ashamed to confess that I had three accidents in the short space of four years.

I will come to this accident presently but let me first describe the worst crash, the one that occurred just before I went to Nigeria. This was when I had got a job with The Wellcome Foundation and I had arranged to sell my car, a Cortina GT, to someone in London. We had agreed that he would pick the car up in Heathrow Terminal 3. I would meet him in check-in, and we would go and inspect the vehicle and complete the transaction. I was going to go down to London on the Saturday night, but I set off for Shrewsbury, where there was a party I had been invited to the day before. My new wife Ann was following me in her sportscar, a rather lovely new blue Triumph Spitfire which Ann's indulgent father had bought for her. We were travelling along the A5 between Oswestry and Shrewsbury when a car travelling in the opposite direction came racing down the middle of the road and swung in front of me. I stood on the brakes but unfortunately I knew we were going to collide. Time stood still, as they say, and I felt I had enough time to make a decision as to whether I would hit this car in the rear, in the front, or amidships. Time does not really stand still of course, and I hit him right between the driver's and rear passenger's doors.

I had a good friend who was a lawyer and I got him to come to the scene just as the police were measuring distances and examining tyre marks and so forth. He supervised these procedures carefully, which stood me in good stead later, because an initial allegation was that I was engaged in a race with the sportscar behind me. I was not racing Ann, of course. We were making our way sensibly to the party in Shrewsbury, where we planned to spend the night before I proceeded down to London.

There were four people in the car that I hit. One had severe head injuries; one had internal injuries and one died, sadly. The driver, who was said to have been drinking heavily, escaped unhurt. He had returned from army service abroad and his father had bought him a Mini, which I believe he might have been driving for the first time. I suppose he was showing off for his friends on what he must have assumed was a quiet country road.

For my part, I broke my sternum on the steering wheel as, of course, these were the days before compulsory seat restraints. I also broke a couple of ribs and damaged my knees, which inevitably smashed into the dashboard. The engine block ended up under the passenger seat beside me. My car was a fairly substantial model, the Cortina GT, and I was not travelling at any great speed because it was raining, and Ann was travelling behind me. Nevertheless, the impact drove this heavy chunk of metal right through to the passenger compartment, which is a scary thought.

Though I would not call myself a petrol head, I was always interested in cars and, as a treat for myself, I had bought my first car, a brand-new Hillman Imp in my last year in Cardiff. It was a crazy machine with all sorts of design faults which I wish I had known about at the time. For instance, the tyre pressures were 38psi in the back and 15 psi in the front. This should give one an idea of the instability of that model. Nevertheless, I bought a second Imp. The first Hillman Imp lasted about six months and was replaced by another Imp for about four months Then I acquired a Ford Cortina, an ex-rep's car. This was during my time in Bradford doing my Masters degree, and also, as I have said, working as a locum in various pharmacies, Because I was earning well by now, I decided to upgrade. I had set my eyes on a Lotus Cortina, which was regarded as a prestigious vehicle in the late sixties and early seventies because it featured an engine designed by Colin Chapman of Lotus. I also had some money, because my insurance company had written off the previous Cortina, but I was still young, and I was unable to get insurance for such a high-performance vehicle. Accordingly, I settled for a Cortina GT.

Three accidents in four years. All of which ended my cars' brief existence on earth. One car, I am happy to say, was retired with full honours. The first accident took place when I was travelling to a pharmacy meeting in Rhyl. There is a nasty stretch of road, winding downhill, and there were a lot of leaves around. If you've got a meagre fifteen pounds pressure in the front tyres, you do not have great roadholding. Going round a sharp bend I lost control and hit a tree halfway up before dropping back down to the ground. I was incredibly lucky in that the windscreen did not smash. Instead, it flew out whole and I promptly followed it, flying through the aperture like a trapeze artist leaving his swing. Still not quite apprehending what had happened, I found myself rolling and rolling down a bank. Amazingly, I was completely unhurt.

The second accident occurred as I was returning home from work in Ruthin. Obviously, one does not want to smash into anybody, but I consider myself particularly unlucky in that the person whose car I hit was a local magistrate. Again, it was on a bend, and he was in a Rover 2000, a very sturdy vehicle, which emerged practically unscathed form the collision. My Imp, on the other hand, did not fare so well. It had to be put on the back of a lorry and taken to its last resting place. I did not, and still do not, consider myself to be a bad driver or even an unlucky driver. I am aware, however, that speed was perhaps an issue for me. I never drank and drove, though a lot of people did in those benighted days. If I was out with friends who had cars but still consumed copious amounts of alcohol, I was happy to drive them home from the pub.

I did drink if I was without my car, of course. You might think that, as a student, one could not afford to do so very regularly but a pint of Brains bitter was one shilling and two pence, or 6p in today's money. It was not strong stuff, however, probably about three percent alcohol, unlike some of the strong lagers you can get today. Some people could drink ten pints of the stuff, though I probably only ever managed eight pints.

The pub that all the Pharmacy students frequented was called The Criterion. It has now changed its name to The Owain Glyndwr. All the different departments at university had their own favourite pub. I probably went a couple of nights mid-week and twice or three times over the weekend.

In my first year our landlady used to cook for us. In the second year, when we were in Howard Gardens, you had to book a meal if you wished the landlady to cook for you. Sadly, she was no great artist in the kitchen and would buy the cheapest joint of meat she could possibly find. I must have had dozens and dozens of lamb's hearts, the occasional beef heart, lots of liver and bacon, which some people loved. I did not count myself one of their number. She was a stickler for punctuality too, so if I missed my evening meal. I would buy a rather substantial meat pie from a pie stall – such things were commonplace sixty years ago. Also, and this will not come as any great surprise, after a night's revels my friends and I would go to the Tiger Bay area of Cardiff, which boasted a plethora of Indian restaurants. We behaved very badly. The food was highly spiced, and I was unused to these flavours, so I did not enjoy these late-night meals much. There would be various extras on the table, such as coconut, peppers, tomatoes etcetera, and I saw some red items which I took to be tomatoes. I promptly downed a handful. They were chillies, of course. I never made that mistake again.

I could afford to eat out because I was in receipt of a full grant, due to the fact that I had a state scholarship and therefore my family was not subjected to means testing. In addition to this state scholarship, I received money through the J. T. Edwards Scholarship, J. T. Edwards being some long forgotten ancient benefactor. It did not amount to a fortune, less than £320 per annum, but my father would also help out. Often when I went back to Carrog he would give me a ten-pound note, or even twenty pounds, though I do not remember seeing a twenty-pound note till some time later. Digs cost me £2-13-0, which would come to less than fifty pounds for the year, bearing in mind that we only paid for the 30 weeks of term time. And that was for full board!

I mentioned earlier that I managed to get myself elected President of The Welsh Pharmaceutical Students Association. I am proud of some of my efforts, because I achieved quite a lot, I think, even down to initiating a Swansea branch of the society. The role had a social aspect and some cultural and educational elements. For these latter I would invite speakers to talk on non-academic aspects of pharmacy work, such as contraception, which was not very well covered in the university curriculum. Thus, I would get a man in from Durex to talk to us. This was the era of free love and oral contraception was beginning to be readily available but the medical reps who would come in and furnish us with free samples of their wares were always welcome.

As far as social aspects of the society were concerned, I felt it would be good to have dances and pop concerts on a regular basis. The refectory of The Welsh College of Advanced Technology, I realised, would make a fine venue because it had a beautiful parquet floor. Together with my *consigliere*, the Entertainments Secretary, I would bully the Dean of The Faculty of Pharmacy, and any other authority figures who might have a say in such matters, into letting us invite bands and hold dances there. We had some very popular evenings and some good bands too, such as The Swinging Blue Jeans. They were an interesting band, or group as we used to call such musical acts, because they were the people who first invited The Beatles to perform in Hamburg. We all know what happened after that. The Swinging Blue Jeans had a top ten hit, and famously had a punch up with The Rolling Stones over ownership of a ballpoint pen being used to sign autographs at the recording of the first *Top of the Pops* TV programme. Their big hit was 'Hippy Hippy Shake', but they were not hippies as such; more devotees of Presley's pelvic thrusting, I guess. I believe they may still be performing as a group. Sorry, band.

A chap I shared digs with in my first year was a musician and electronics whiz kid. He played guitar with, or perhaps truer to say, alongside, The Blue Jeans. He was called Charlie DeSchoolmeister. Unfortunately, he did not have a great voice and his musical career did not last very long. I played with Charlie for a little while. Indeed, it was he who taught me the main chords and how to fingerpick so that I could attempt the folk songs which were still popular in the early sixties. I never played publicly, however, apart from those times I played in parties and so forth.

In my second year I was lodged in Howard Gardens, which is to this day a very vibrant student area of Cardiff. There was a real character there called Danny. He was a Merthyr boy doing his year's teacher training certificate and he had very little academic work to do, so he entertained himself by trying to prevent the rest of us from doing any meaningful work. He was something of an anarchist. He obtained a teaching position in London, and he was up against thirteen- and fourteen-year-olds who were not too enamoured of the educational system. On one occasion a pupil threatened him with violence and Danny got hold of the miscreant and, shall we say, restrained him. The boy's father came to the school to wreak some sort of revenge. Danny was calmness personified. 'That's okay,' he said, 'you can beat me up if you like. But I'm telling you, you beat me up and I'll make the rest of your son's time in school truly terrible. I will smash him to a warm pulp! It's up to you; you beat me up and I'll beat your boy up!' It was a typical Merthyr response to a threat of violence.

Danny had spent a fair amount of time in boxing booths and had, if not a love, certainly a fondness for pugilism. I recall one time when we were about to catch the train back from Bristol to Cardiff, a little worse for wear, as usual, when a gang of youths approached, clearly intent on some type of fisticuffs. All of a sudden, a woman appeared on the platform shouting, 'The police are coming, the police are

30

coming!' The thugs ran off, but Danny held his ground and called for them to come back. He was not a man to fear anything.

Life calmed down somewhat subsequently. In my third year of university I stayed with a Mr and Mrs Carter in Canton. They were nice, quiet, respectable people who lived in the upstairs flat. I shared the downstairs flat with a an equally quiet, respectable young man called Maurice, who coincidentally retired to Brecon, as of course I did some years ago. It is strange to recall the closeness we doubtless had all those years ago and reflect that, though vivid then, our friendship is now only a faded fragment in a corner of the highly detailed tapestry of one's life.

After finishing my degree, as I have said, I went to work in a pharmacy in Ruthin. This involved turning up for work five days a week and checking and restocking shelves, and not just for medications, but all the other sundries sold there. I hated this menial work. Even when I actually performed some pharmaceutical tasks, I found the task of merely dispensing Mrs Evans' or Mrs Jones' tablets a particularly unedifying and unstimulating way of earning a living or demonstrating anything about the skills I had learned at university.

The work one does in a pharmacy is measured by the number of scripts you dole out. It is not quite as tedious as assembly line work, for you are compelled to do a little bit of thinking, such as deciding if a particular medicine can be taken in conjunction with another treatment. But when I was working in Bradford as a locum, for instance, and taking evening shifts, which would be 5.30 to 9.00 pm, I would be exhausted. There were a lot of non-English speaking customers because of the huge influx of Asians to that area and I had to use sign language and hold up a number of fingers to indicate the number of tablets and their daily frequency. Perhaps I should have tried to learn a smattering of Bengali, Urdu, or Pashtu, but I do not know how much that would have helped, even if I had had the diligence and the linguistic ability to do so. Not all of the people I dealt with would necessarily speak the main language of their native country. It would have been like learning Spanish to communicate with people who mainly spoke Catalan. Or even more dramatically,

31

trying to talk to people in the Basque country who will only speak Euskara.

The problem with pharmacy is that you get very bright students who pass difficult exams and then have to enter a field (or a cesspit, as I sometimes think of it) where there is no intellectual stimulation whatsoever. A script comes in, you read it, and you label a tube of ointment or a bottle of tablets. For thirty-seven hours a week you do this in the company of sales assistants and fellow pharmacists who, sometimes within ten years of this repetitive work, have become hollowed out and have lost all art of talking about ideas or anything other than the minutiae of pharmacy. I was studying finance and economics at the same time as this locum work, and I wanted to think about and discuss a range of more exhilarating topics.

After the tedium of my year working in Boots, I found my Masters course very interesting. You would go into university on a Monday morning and be given a piece of paper with a task on it. You had to produce a file two days later. 'You have access to all sorts of books and papers,' the tutors would say, 'so we want you to imagine that the year is 1953 and someone has found a way of creating square section steel tubing. What can you do with this?'

Obviously, one would consider the various applications: domestic, industrial, or military, for instance. But then came the issue of a pricing policy. It did not matter what answers were generated because the point of such exercises was to make the students think creatively. I loved such intellectual work. I had something called a Rapidograph pen, which was a single stylus writing implement filled with indelible ink, often used by architects. I could not type, but I settled on this implement because it could draw very thin lines of constant width and I could include graphs or tiny diagrams as I wrote out my ideas.

At midday on the Wednesday I would produce my results, having worked tirelessly for forty-eight hours. I was awarded very high marks, but sometimes I was so fatigued I scarcely knew what I had written. I think my successes may partly have been the result of my competitive nature. I would cast an eye over my fellow students and consider whether I was better than them or not. I learned quickly to access library resources, rather than spend time chatting about the task, or about where we were going that night. In other words, I applied myself rigorously. I would be disappointed if I scored less than ninety percent on these tasks.

Rather arrogantly, I felt that I was probably intellectually superior to the men who were teaching me, as I had once done about Boliog, the Physics teacher at school. I even found the dissertation a very straightforward task. Nevertheless, because I was paying the course fees myself, I had a dread of failure and, there was one area of my Finance studies that I did find very difficult to grasp, largely because there was almost n o teaching of the topic. It concerned something called Modigliani's Principles. This Neo-Keynesian thesis is of interest, of course, but I fear not to me at that moment in time. I had to sit an exam on this topic, and I forced myself to stay the full three-hour duration, but I hardly knew what to write. This caused me to be fearful about graduating, because one had to achieve over fifty percent in all papers, and I doubted I had even written enough sense to get ten percent. Whoever marked my paper was, thank goodness, either full of the milk of human kindness or was extremely inebriated, it has to be said. I passed the module and therefore the course, and my expectations for what I might get out of this year's study were set to be met.

Despite this glitch I had always prided myself on possessing good exam technique, being able to quickly deduce where the most marks would be allocated and, when unsure which side of an argument to pursue in an answer, argue cogently on either side. I also tried to ensure that my answers were easy to mark, with clear precise writing. I never failed to answer questions, even when short of time, because I would cover the ground in note form if I were pressed. I had a theory that I could make the examiner think that I actually knew more than I did know. Perception is key and awareness of one's audience is also vital. This understanding was something I carried into my business life, needless to say.

At the end of the course there was a hiring fair. All the details of the postgrad students were sent out to relevant pharmaceutical companies. Four firms were interested in meeting me, but strangely enough Wellcome was not one of them. The positions I was offered were all overseas jobs in big Pharma companies, for instance in Greece and in The Philippines. Wellcome had not even attended the hiring fair, but they must have received the student profiles because a chap called Harry Mendelsohn, the Head of HR there, approached my father. He telephoned him, having got my home number from my file, and said that he was sure that I would receive lots of offers but that the company for me was definitely Wellcome. He gave my father his number and recommended that I think about this opportunity. That night I spoke to my father, and he said, 'Obviously they're keen for you to join them so you'd be wise to consider it.'

I went through a series of interviews, and I was told that the company would like to employ me. They were not offering silly money exactly, but it was double what I had been earning at Boots. Plainly the amount does not sound very impressive these days, but it was 1969 and sixteen thousand pounds was a more than fair annual salary. By comparison, someone starting in the teaching profession at that time could expect an annual salary of eighteen hundred pounds.

Though remuneration is always a key factor when you get a job, the main attraction to me of working for Wellcome was the opportunity for foreign travel. I would be based in the United Kingdom, but I would travel to the Middle East, stay somewhere for a week or so then come back and report my findings. One thing I realised was that I was proficient at accounting. This was to prove very useful when I was sent out to Africa to help a man called Jimmy Mackie, who was an old India hand who had been with the company for years. He was more than comfortable in India, but he realised that his pension would be enhanced of he went to a place like Nigeria for a few years. He was told that he would not have to do any heavy lifting because the company would send a sprog out to do the real work. That sprog was me.

The Middle Eastern countries I visited were Kuwait, Jordan and Lebanon. My task was to look for gaps in the market in these territories and then put together a plan as to how we could fill those gaps. I was basically employed not on the medical side of the company, but in dealing with consumer products like sweeteners, worm medicines, prophylactics and so on. There was a market research tool available to the company through the agency of The IMS – International Medical Services – which would target a representative sample of pharmacies in any country and require them to return invoices indicating what products and how much of them had been sold over a certain period. Nevertheless, I thought there would be no harm doing personal research too, and I found it interesting work, walking around the various pharmacies, finding out what sold well, what was not on offer. Though I had begun my career as a pharmacist, basically for these early days I was a market researcher.

I think Wellcome liked what I was doing. The company was not advertising its products in any of these Middle Eastern countries and the golden rule is to ensure you have a good distribution system in place first, then advertise your wares. Wellcome were slow to grasp this fundamental principle and I think they were surprised, and perhaps gratified, that they had a kid telling them what to do. Get some reps out there, I was insisting, get your stuff on the shelves! Then you can advertise and start getting the stuff *off* the shelves.

The posting to Nigeria was partly a reward for the 'Can Do' attitude I was exhibiting in generating sales in the Middle East. The people I was replacing in West Africa were not, shall we say, the sharpest knives in the drawer. Jimmy Mackie, for instance, did not have a clue about promoting sales. He was head honcho in Nigeria, married to a colonel's daughter, don't ye know. She thought that Africa was the last place on earth she and her husband should end up in. 'The servants here are absolutely awful,' she would say. You can probably hear her tone of voice and her Received Pronunciation here on the page.

When I landed in Nigeria, I started off in the airport hotel in Ikeja. Later on, when I got married, I was found a little bungalow. I say 'little', but it did have three bedrooms and air conditioning, though that seemed to expel nothing but warm air. It also had servants' quarters at the rear. These being still colonial rather than post-colonial times, I had a cook, a steward, a gardener, a driver and a 'small boy', which was the title of the steward's assistant. It all might seem rather excessive now, this array of people dedicated to the service of one company man, but we were, I suppose, offering significant employment opportunities to men and women who would otherwise find work hard to get. Nigerians did not mind working for white people, though they hated working for their own countrymen. or countrywomen, I should say, for it is true that rich Nigerians, especially rich Nigerian women, treated their staff very badly.

It is important to understand that the domestic and social systems of a country like Nigeria were very different from the systems we are accustomed to in the UK. Families are invariably extended units, where children are raised by uncles, aunts, cousins and grandparents, as well as parents. Because resources are shared between such large networks those people who are not related, namely the serving classes, are regarded as parasites.

I should try and describe what it was like to be waited upon, like some sort of aristocrat, while I was living in Ikeja. In the morning, my steward would knock on my door. 'Tea, sir,' he would say. I would take a sip then go to breakfast, which was admittedly quite a modest affair. At this stage 'Madame' would get up. The driver would come in to collect my briefcase and be handed it by my steward. He would carry this precious cargo out to the car, which he would already have cleaned and checked for correct tyre pressure (thankfully more than 15psi). Once the engine was running, I would appear and get into the back of the car and be driven sedately to my place of work. This was a couple of miles away on a big trading estate. One should remember that I was not an aristocrat from the Home Counties by birth. Rather, I was the son of a civil servant and a schoolteacher, and my origins were in a small village in North Wales.

After work I would meet up with the ex-pats employed in the other companies based on the trading estate. My wife Ann had acquired a horse and we went to a riding club at about 5.30. She would ride for an hour or so while I partook of a libation or two with employees of Dunlop and the other big multinationals. Ann would join us after her ride, and we would have a further drink or two before returning to a meal prepared by the cook.

Ann did not have a job in Nigeria, but she enjoyed reading and playing Mah Jong with the ladies she met. It was all as if we had been transported to The Raj in the twenties and thirties. Even down to the esoteric little things that people missed from their homeland. In Jimmy Mackie's case it was packets of Knorr soup and tins of butter from Harrods. He was a dapper man who I rather think could have been played by someone like David Niven, if his life had been committed to film. He had asked me by telex to bring out the packet soups and the prestigious butter when I travelled to Ikeja, and I dutifully did so.

The following week Ann and I were invited to dinner at Jimmy's. Ladies were to wear evening dress, but Jimmy informed me that he would be in 'Red Sea rig', which was clearly an indication that I should also be so attired. I think he may have been trying to catch me out, but luckily, I understood the term, which refers to the etiquette of wearing dinner suit trousers with a cummerbund, dress shirt and tie but no jacket. This regalia was originally a naval concept for officers serving in the sweltering heat of the Middle East, but it was soon adopted by diplomats in Jeddah and then by British Business Group employees.

On the appointed evening we arrived, Ann in a beautiful evening dress and I in my Red Sea rig, and we were served sherry by one of Jimmy's staff. Then we sat down to what we imagined would be a fine, multi-course dinner. Maureen Mackie sat at one end of the table and Jimmy, her husband, on the other. There was one other couple in attendance too. Maureen had her little brass bell in front of her and, when she deemed that we were all comfortable seated, she gave it a tinkle. There were some shuffling noises from the kitchen, but no food appeared. There was a slightly more adamant tinkling of the little bell. Once again nothing appeared. Maureen disappeared into the kitchen and came back to announce, 'We will start with the main course.'

Eventually it transpired that she had given the packets of Knorr soup I had brought over from the UK to her steward, who had shown these mysterious items to the gardener. The gardener had had a lightbulb moment and taken the packets out to vegetable garden and planted the contents there with a stick through the empty packet denoting what was in each row. Presumably, he hoped he would, in due course, be cultivating mixed vegetables, oxtails and mushrooms.

There was another tale from the Jimmy Mackie dinner party days, but I think it is probably apocryphal and is more likely just a well-known West African tale mocking the misunderstandings of Anglo-Nigerian communication. When an important personality was due to come out from London to Nigeria the ex-pat wives would vie to outshine each other in terms of the hospitality that was offered. On one particular occasion it was decided that a suckling pig would be the highlight of an elaborate dinner. The steward was told that a very special guest was expected, so the food was to be served through the serving hatch. The hostess forgot she had told him this when it was subsequently decided that the centre piece was a whole piglet, but the steward, a punctilious servant, had not forgotten. The bell to announce the arrival of the food was tinkled and an arm and a leg appeared, thrust through the hatch. To top it all the steward appeared with an apple in his mouth, though I think this embellishment proves the apocryphal nature of the story.

Chapter 3 *The Wellcome Foundation*

When I'm fishing, I feel guilty that I'm not working, and when I'm working, I feel guilty that I'm not fishing

Raymond Carver

I joined The Wellcome Foundation in October 1968. At first, I was making trips to the Middle East and, as I have related, conducting market research for consumer products. I was rewarded for my efforts with an appointment to the company's office in Nigeria. Unfortunately, the serious car accident I have described earlier delayed my departure for Africa. I was recuperating at home for several months and this delayed my taking up my role there.

I got married in 1970. I remember proposing to Ann by phone from a public phone box in Nigeria (which was not very romantic, I know) on Valentine's Day 1969. She accepted my proposal, but we had a somewhat stormy relationship for the next few months and on New Year's Eve 1969 we decided to break up. In the early days of January we made up again, and what seemed like a firm resolve to go our own separate ways turned out to be a mere spat, probably the result of pre-wedding nerves. We were both doubtless a lot more nervous about our impending move to Africa than we cared to admit. We were not afraid as such, more aware that we would be out of touch with family and friends for quite a while. We married on January 10th, a very cold day, I recall.

I had met Ann in a dance in Corwen some years before. I had just finished my exams at Cardiff, and it was late September 1964. I knew most of the young women who went to these weekend dances, but Ann's was a new face to me. I approached her and said, 'Are you with the band?' She was quite hurt, and I had to excuse myself. But I plucked up courage and offered to take her back to mid-Wales the following evening, for she was staying with a friend in Corwen that night. She lived in a little village called Llanfair Caereinion, near Welshpool, which is a good hour's drive along narrow country roads. She did not have a car in those days, so she was grateful for the offer. Shortly afterwards her father bought her a new Triumph Spitfire and we became that rarity in those times, a two-car couple.

Ann was working as a physiotherapist in the mid-Wales health service, but we stayed in touch throughout the time I was in Bradford, with me dutifully telephoning her every night. She had to give up her work, of course, when we moved to Nigeria, there being no chance of a work permit for her there. I was on a 10/2 split, which is to say I worked for ten months and then was on leave for two months. Later on, having achieved a few brownie points, I was put on a 5/1 split, which was a lot more palatable.

Ann settled very well in Nigeria because she loved reading, and when she discovered Agatha Christie, she began demolishing the whole oeuvre, at a rate of a novel every two days perhaps. Where we were living, in Ikeja, was also a good place to make friends. One couple, Lyn and Pat, were from South Wales so we had an instant connection; another couple, Trevor and Ann Salmon, hailed from Yorkshire, but we did not hold that against them. Dennis Thornley, another friend, married a Thai woman called Lek, whom he had met while working in Bangkok. he was an ex-Fleet Air Arm pilot. Naturally, they brought a set of new and interesting experiences to our social gatherings. Dennis was actually the archetypal English gentleman. I think he may have felt that his present line of work, making cheap jewellery for the masses with a company called Fimcon, was somewhat infradig after his rather more glamorous career as a pilot, but he did not admit it. There was a huge market for chains, bracelets, and such items, and due to the Biafran War there was a high import tax on luxury goods. By manufacturing inside Nigeria, Fimcon had the entire market to themselves.

Ann and I enjoyed our life in Nigeria, though halfway through my first tour we found ourselves absolutely exhausted. I remember looking at my diary and realising that we had been out living it up for forty consecutive nights. Something of a contrast to forty nights in the desert, you might say. I worked hard in the day, and I socialised hard at night; something you can do in your twenties with thoughtless ease.

During my second tour in Nigeria Ann joined the Saddle Club, where she enjoyed her horse riding, but we also invested in a speedboat, which we moored in Lagos, about twenty miles from Ikeja. I never learned to swim, and I had no experience with boats, but I employed a Boat Boy at the harbour to look after the craft. I would normally carry a toolbox containing anything I might need in the event of any sort of breakdown, but on the one occasion when something did go wrong, I discovered that this local lad had forgotten to put the toolbox aboard.

We wanted to go to a place called Bar Beach but when I started the engine, a Johnson Sea Horse 40hp and a beast of a thing, the propeller hit the sand and a metal pin snapped We found ourselves in grave danger of floating out to sea; me, Ann and our dog floating helpless in the Atlantic. Luckily, we had not drifted any real distance before another boat nearby saw that we were in difficulty and offered us a tow back to where we were going. I would have been reasonably happy if we could have just hugged the coastline, but we had to go out beyond the mile long mole, or stone breakwater, that jutted out to sea. The rowlock that I had tied the tow rope to then broke and I began to get worried, but another couple came along and threw us a rope. Ann was concerned that if this rope broke it might put this couple in trouble too, for they had two small children with them. There was no further drama, however, and we managed to make it back to Lagos and the only lasting damage was the severe sunburn I suffered on my back because of the heat and the sea breeze.

I was very grateful to the couple who had helped us, and I thought the least I could do was to buy them a meal to demonstrate my gratitude. We went home and changed and met them for a nice dinner at a place called Apapa, but the experience at sea was a chastening one and I vowed not to repeat it. I blame my sheer inexperience with boats. Instead of trying to be towed, as if we were

41

in a car, we should have lashed our boats together side by side.

One of the other dramatic incidents that took place was when someone tried to grab Ann's horse as she was out riding with her group of girls one day. They had gone to a very pleasant orange grove, which was out in the bush, but as they were coming back a man appeared from nowhere and seemed to be trying to steal her horse. There was no real danger because they were a large group and this was a single interloper, but it did stress the need to be wary when outside one's normal environment.

I would not want to suggest that life was filled with drama and danger. There were funny moments involving local people too. For instance, my driver, a man called Amos, was not a man overburdened by great intelligence, but he was diligent about his work. I was due to have a new car, a white Peugeot, delivered by SCOA Motors. Amos came running in as soon as he took delivery of the car. 'Sir, sir, the car need petrol!' he gasped.

I knew that any new car coming straight from the garage would have been filled with fuel so I tried to reassure him that he must be mistaken.

'Come on, Amos,' I said, as I sat in the car and turned the ignition key. 'Look, the needle has gone straight up to F.'

'Yes sir,' he said. 'F. It mean finish.'

'Okay, Amos,' I said, 'if F is for finished, what does E stand for?'

'E stand for enough, sir.'

I do not wish to sound patronising as I recall the naivety of men like Amos. There was far too much patronising of people who were simply not as well versed in some of the matters that we Westerners took for granted. I deplored it when I saw such condescension then and I deplore it now. I liked Amos and I am very flattered that when he and his wife had a little boy, they decided to call him Jones.

My day-to-day work in Nigeria was running a direct distribution service. We had a number of Volkswagen Combi vans which left the depot at the beginning of the month with around a thousand pounds worth of medical supplies on board. They would return at the end of the month with the cash. Some of the better drivers returned after a couple of weeks and hence doubled their take home pay. I had to ensure that the van operation was properly run. Dealing with cash and product in a country that was at the time full of dishonest people was not the easiest of tasks. I succeeded in overcoming the threat of theft and corruption by employing salesman only after their families had given me a thousand pounds as a warrant of the driver's honesty.

Thinking again about that period of my life and the difficulties that drivers faced, I remember how bad traffic was, even after the Biafran War had finished. I had to do a fair amount of driving myself and in some ways I consider myself lucky to be alive, having been witness to some awful atrocities of war.

I used to have to travel to Biafra, where most of the fighting in that terrible conflict took place. In order to understand the politics of the country one needs to apprehend the ethnic and tribal makeup of the country. There are a good number of tribes, each with their own language, customs and culture, but three major ethnic groups predominate. One of these, the Ibo, who were the Christian contingent to the East, occupied an area known as Biafra. Their attempt to secede from the Nigerian federal government in 1967 was the cause of the Biafran War, which was waged for nearly three years. Their main enemies were the Yoruba, who, despite their Muslim and Christian beliefs, were a warlike people to the West and North. The third grouping was the mainly Muslim Hausa-Fulani tribe to the North. The Hausa-Fulani had an elite who were good at organising; the Ibo were strong and bright people; the Yoruba had few ethnic traits that I could admire, however.

Mercenaries were important in the Biafran War because neither the Biafrans nor the Nigerians had much experience of fighting. Indeed, they had served more as a police force than an army up to the outbreak of the conflict. A man called Steiner claimed to have fought for Biafra for idealistic reasons, saying the Ibo people were the victims of genocide, but the American journalist Ted Morgan mocked his claims, describing Steiner as a militarist who simply craved war because killing was the only thing he knew how to do well. Journalist and novelist Frederick Forsyth has spoken about Taffy Williams, a Welsh mercenary who rose to the rank of major.

Taffy claimed that he was inspired by the bravery of the Biafran soldiers, 'I've seen a lot of Africans at war,' he said, 'but there's nobody to touch these people. Give me 10,000 Biafrans for six months, and we'll build an army that would be invincible on this continent. I've seen men die in this war who would have won the Victoria Cross in another context.'

My own experience of the horrors of this civil war stays imprinted on my mind. On one occasion I actually witnessed the Federal Third Army come down the east side of the River Niger to try and cut off the Biafran forces. They had seen convoys before and knew that there would be seventy or eighty green non-armoured sixteen-wheeler articulated lorries, each containing about 150 soldiers. At the rear there would be a few petrol tankers and leading the procession an armoured car or two and a few jeeps containing the officers. The Federal force attacked the jeeps and the Federal officers took to their heels without even ordering their men to disembark from the troop carriers. Then there was a massacre of the helpless troops, the Biafran soldiers going up and down the stalled convoy with machine guns as if they were shooting fish in a barrel. There was no question of taking prisoners. The Federal forces were supported by Russia and Britain; Britain because of our oil interests, the Russians because they loved to interfere wherever they could. The Biafrans, of course, were supported by the French, again because of oil interests. Though there had been some exploration on the Cameroon side of the country, the oil wells were mostly situated in Biafra, so it was natural enough for that community to want to retain control of their valuable resource.

The politics of this situation are appalling of course, but from my own point of view, purely as a businessman, it was important to gain a good working knowledge of the tribal system, which is heavily reliant on family networks. Thus, I would always appoint a storekeeper who was from one of the less privileged sections of society, because he would be less likely to want to seek employment opportunities for large numbers of his family. This might seem a trivial matter, but it made a big difference if one was running a substantial business. It was a good example of the old British divide and rule principle.

Wellcome's manufacturing centre was in the West and the distribution centre in the East, in Biafra. I had to go to the bank every Thursday and arrange for our London bank to send enough money for me to pay the workers' wages. Although the work I am describing was mainly organisation and admin I was still a pharmacist at heart and when I had a look through Wellcome's full catalogue I saw that we were making things of interest to the military. One prime example was gas gangrene anti-serum, which was in great demand during the war. If you are fighting in dirty, muddy conditions and you are hit, the bullet is prone to take a fragment of cloth with it and the victim is highly likely to contract gas gangrene. The only remedy is an anti-serum, and the production of such a treatment involves finding a horse and bleeding it to produce the serum. If one thinks about it, the most valuable horses in the world are not the winners of the Derby or The Grand National, but some rather less exalted beasts in a stable in Beckenham, capable of making the anti-serum which will save soldiers' lives.

The logistics of getting serum that has to be stored at under five degrees centigrade to where it is needed mean that it has to be flown into somewhere with a cold store and then transported to where the army has cold storage. You have to demonstrate to the purchasing body that the serum has not exceeded this five-degree temperature at any time on its journey from the United Kingdom. I succeeded in setting up a distribution network. Then one day a big man literally kicked my office door open. He was not wearing any military insignia because he was a Polish mercenary doctor working for the Federal Army. He said, 'I've been sent here to shoot you.'

I was aghast.

'My team worked for three days and nights,' he went on, 'amputating soldiers' limbs and administering the gas gangrene you sent us. There was not a single survivor!'

I said, 'You can shoot me now, but you'll still have your problem.' I invited him to come with me to inspect the cold store. 'This is where there was an initial temperature change,' I stated, 'when we took the serum out to send to your cold store.' He looked

45

dubious. 'let's go down to the army store and look at the signals,' I said.

We did so and then it became perfectly clear that the medication had left our store in a good state, but it had not been delivered straight away. Rather, it had been left sitting on the airport runway for about three weeks. I said, 'You need to come with me immediately. We'll go and see Brigadier Austin Peters.' Peters was the Head of AFMS, the medical services branch of the armed forces. We talked to the brigadier about what had happened, and he asked us what he should do about this wastage.

The Polish doctor spoke up. 'Give this man,' he said clasping me on the shoulder, 'a contract to deliver medicines directly to the front.' At which the brigadier took out his notepad. 'Okay,' he said, 'how much will it cost?' Of course, I had no idea, but I could not admit that. It was a case of think of a number, multiply by ten, double it and then add a few noughts. I said,' It will be very much more expensive than what it has cost you thus far.' I handed him a slip of paper with the number. He looked at it and, without batting an eyelid, took out a pad and scribbled a few words. 'There you are, that's your order,' he said.

The value of that shipment was about five hundred thousand pounds. Now I was faced with the problem of figuring out how to get the stuff to military units in advanced positions. I knew I needed to conduct an experiment or two. I had no refrigerated vehicles, but I did have plenty of Volkswagen Combi vans. I thought that if I lined them with polystyrene tiles and put cold blocks in the back of the vans it might give us time to transport the stock without the temperature rising too much. I calculated we had about thirty-six hours between pick-up and delivery where we could hold the temperature below five degrees. As an experiment, I put temperature sensors in the load and measured how well the insulation worked. I then drove two vans to Enugu, the capital of Eastern Nigeria, where there was a bridge over the River Niger that had been destroyed. There, I saw a sight that not many people have ever witnessed: a huge static convoy of sixteen-wheeler lorries chartered by Oxfam and carrying vital food supplies, such as stockfish. The convoy must have stretched for five miles, but nothing was moving. Indeed, there had been no movement for weeks and months. The sad reason was that somebody had neglected to bribe the army in order to get the supplies across the river.

I knew I could not wait in such a queue because of the fragility of my cargo. I had to find a solution. I drove upstream for a few miles until I got to a village whose main industry involved the collection of sand from the bottom of the river for use in the construction trade. The sand was transported in barges that plied their way up and down the river. Knowing that ready cash was vital for the purposes of persuading locals to help me in circumstances such as these, I invariably wore a money belt stuffed with banknotes strapped to my chest. I approached the head man of the village and said, 'I want you to tie two barges together. Lash them properly.' He was willing to do so when I offered him a wad of notes. We unloaded the Combi vans, put the empty vehicles onto the sand barges, reloaded them and headed downstream till we could find a road.

That night we arrived at Enugu, where the main Field Ambulance Unit was, and where there were refrigeration facilities, so I knew my cargo was safe. Approaching the field hospital, I smelled the gas gangrene. It was a sickly, awful smell. We unloaded the vans, got the temperature charts, handed them over, got the necessary signature from the receiving officer and headed back. It had been something of a guess that this enterprise might take about thirty-six hours, but I had been accurate in my calculations, fortunately.

The vans wore the company's livery and logo, so I thought we might be in danger of being set upon by renegades. It was not at all far-fetched to think that we could be shot, just for our Combis, now that they had served their purpose. I decided to destroy them, not wishing them to be stolen and used for any nefarious purposes. I used to smoke in those days, so I decided to put my lighter to better use than helping damage my lungs. I ignited the petrol tanks of the two vehicles and retired quickly. Now, of course, I had the problem of getting back to Ikeja.

Planes did come into Enugu airport, but there were no civil

flights, only government aircraft. In those days I wore long white socks with a pencil slotted down inside one of them, as was the fashion. I also wore white shirts with epaulettes. I thought I might be readily confused with flight crew so I went up to a pilot just as if I were a fellow airman and said, 'Hey, could I grab a lift back to Lagos?' This pilot might have been taking a huge risk allowing me to board his plane, because I could have been a terrorist. But a white shirt and epaulettes did wonders for the British over the years and once again they proved effective. Actually, anyone who has seen the movie *Catch Me If You Can* will realise that it is not as difficult as it might seem to impersonate being a pilot. You just have to have the confidence, or the impudence, I should say, to carry it off.

The plane was a twin-engine Beechcraft, a very popular light aircraft used for business as well as military purposes. It was picking up a cargo of used banknotes from the East, so I found myself sitting on mailbags full of dirty unusable cash. I felt there may have been some sort of metaphor here to do with the moneys to be made out of the tragedy of war, but it was not one I chose to pursue at this time.

In 1972 Ann and I were back in the United Kingdom and based in Berkhamsted in Hertfordshire. I had made a lot of money for Wellcome by dint of being rather more alert than some of the people around me, so I was shocked when I came back and saw the Personnel manager and he told me I should put my name down on the Hemel Hempstead council housing waiting list. I was not going to do that. Instead, I rented a small house and eventually moved on to Ashridge, a pretty little village to the north of Berkhamsted and home to a well-known management college.

I had done pretty well for Wellcome in the Middle East, as well as in Nigeria, and they later felt it appropriate that they should help me in my search for accommodation. I found a house in Cheddington, a village near Tring, which was within my budget. It was a new build, detached four-bedroom house with a double garage and cost me £12,500. This might seem a very modest sum but in 1972 it was practically double what some people were paying, I suppose. Also, it was the era of the gazumper. The term 'gazumping' is not one that is heard much anymore, but it refers to the

48

phenomenon of people paying more than the asking price for a house. You would think that your offer for a house had been accepted, then you would discover that someone had come along and offered more, leading the vendor to renege on your deal. There was a certain amount of panic buying of property in the early part of the seventies because everyone could see that the housing market was moving so rapidly.

I went to a lawyer friend of mine, David Rimmer, and said, 'David, you've got to help me; I need to buy another house.' I had taken the rather bold step of selling our house in Cheddington for cash. I had nowhere to live now but David told me he knew of a family who were in a desperate situation. They were anxious to complete a sale on their property by the following Friday because they were splitting up and needed to settle their finances with some urgency. They wanted £42,000 for their lovely house in Leighton Buzzard. One of the features that appealed to us was the number of huge sequoia trees it had in the beautiful garden. The vicar in Leighton Buzzard was a keen gardener and had worked in Kew Gardens. He was interested in the science of growing sequoias, which occur naturally in California and Oregon but not normally elsewhere. He succeeded too, hence causing one of the main streets in the town to be renamed Plantation Road. These giant redwoods are impressive trees, and we were lucky enough to have ten of them in our garden when we came to sell up and move on ten years later. The house rose considerably in value during our sojourn there and we sold it for nearly £300,000.

The house had been expensive to purchase in the first place, of course, but I had enough cash for a reasonable deposit and was able to get a mortgage because I was earning a decent salary at Wellcome. Also, at this time I had just started setting up my own company, Agropharm, which was a sort of moonlighting enterprise I had dreamed up with a close friend, Bryan Shand. He was an agronomist and I was, of course, a pharmacist, so we combined our professions for the business name. We based ourselves in a village called Penn, near High Wycombe.

Bryan was one of the best traders I ever met, and we became

good friends as well as business partners. We had both worked in the Middle East and knew how things worked out there. He had a network of agents in various countries in the area, but we decided not to try and compete with Wellcome. Instead, we were happy to trade in a range of commodities. If somebody wanted spare parts for tractors, or tents, or any manner of item really, we would bid for the contract and when we were successful, we ensured that we had a confirmed irrevocable letter of credit. This was as good as cash, and we were able to source whatever was required without having to risk any capital of our own. Admittedly, we sometimes had to adapt the buyer's specifications to what we were able to acquire. but Bryan's experience abroad meant that he knew how to persuade agents to accept modifications, as long as there was a financial inducement for them, naturally.

In my day job, so to speak, I was rather more involved in marketing operations than distribution at this stage in my career. There was a lot of travelling involved, often to Libya because I was regarded as the Libya specialist. At the same time as I was working in Libya, I was journeying back and forth to Nigeria to conduct operations on the veterinary and industrial side of the company's business, having given up the pharmaceutical side of things in favour of animal medicine. Wellcome were producing veterinary products under the name Coooper, McDougall and Robertson, including treatments for ticks and fleas, which were essential for this part of the world. In addition, the industrial side of things involved such things as insecticides, also very important in Africa. I had accepted this move because I felt it was another string to my bow. Now, I had experience in four different industries – in pharmaceuticals, and in products belonging to each of the industrial, consumer and veterinary domains.

It was all extremely hard work. On a fairly regular basis, say every other month, I would threaten to resign from Wellcome, but management came up with a clever strategy to keep me on board, namely by paying me more money. I would show them offers I had received from other pharma companies, and I would say, 'Do you want to match this?' They agreed to do this each time, until I finally ran out of such offers of alternative employment. Then I felt I was trapped, seemingly wired into the company with wires of steel. Or rather, platinum, because that is a more expensive metal.

At one stage the Chairman of The Wellcome Foundation called me in to speak to me. I thought I was going to get some sort of reward for all my efforts. Not so. He said, 'Roger, Africa is a busted flush. We don't need you there anymore. We want you to work in the communist countries instead.' I knew nothing about the geopolitical situation in any of these countries, but that did not seem to matter. 'We think that's where the big money is now,' he said. I told him I did not speak any of the pertinent languages. The Chairman pressed a buzzer on his desk and a woman, a sort of Miss Moneypenny, appeared. 'Book Mr Jones onto a Berlitz Schule course for a month,' he said. Then, turning to me imperiously, 'What language do you want to do?'

I did not fancy my chances with Russian, with its Cyrillic alphabet, so I said tamely, 'German?'

'Done,' he said. 'I'll get someone to send you the details.' He was very much a CAN-DO type of character. Certainly, he was not a man to be crossed in argument. Sadly, when I started work in the communist countries nobody wanted to speak German; everyone wanted to speak English. But I put the hours in, and I could read a contract in German, even if I could not follow a lecture in such a hastily acquired new tongue.

As far as Eastern Europe is concerned, as well as my daily work for Wellcome, I was doing deals with the Russians, who were making a fuel additive called phenothiazine. They had not capitalised upon or evaluated the multiple applications of this substance, but I knew that it could also be used as a vermicide in cattle. There are even applications in a range of human clinical situations, such as in the treatment of schizophrenia and other psychotic disorders. At this time, however, I knew in the right form it would be popular in The United States as an additive to animal feed, because it was relatively cheap and very effective in killing animal worms. Perhaps counter-intuitively, it was effective because it only killed about 98% of the worms; animals fared better when they still had some residual worms, because their own immune systems could remain active in attacking the invaders.

I realised early on that phenothiazine had to be in the form of a very fine powder to work as a vermicide. This meant I had to import Russian shipments and send them to Huddersfield, where I knew a man who could grind the stuff down to the right specification. Agropharm spent roughly £300,000 on my first shipment but was able to sell it on for double that amount. My work with Agropharm had allowed me to build up something of a nest egg for investments such as this, but even if I had not been able to lay my hands on the money there were always investors in the Arab world who would have been interested in being involved. I have to say, it was good money and quickly achieved.

These were exciting times, but I knew that I was sailing pretty close to the wind, so I was happy to avoid any potential trouble with Wellcome by moving to Smith, Kline and French. Looking back over the distance of some decades I am confident that I was probably safe from any real punitive action from management due to the fact that I was aware that Wellcome itself had practices and accounting procedures that might not have borne too close a scrutiny. It was a sort of mutually assured destruction, to coin a phrase.

The chief pharmacist for the Libyan government was someone I had known quite well at university. He was a man called Mohammed Femah and because we had a sort of old boy network, though a Cardiff-based one rather than one sprung from the wells of Eton and Oxbridge, he supplied me with lots of orders. I would only stay in Benghazi for three or four days at a time, so I was not close enough to the Libyan people to fully apprehend what they felt about the tensions between Qaddafi's government and countries in the West, notably The United States. There were serious tensions though, because Libya was promoting an anti-Western ideology and actively supporting rebel groups such as Palestine guerrillas, Philippine Muslims, the Black Panthers and even the IRA. Furthermore, and this was something I was keenly aware of, Qaddafi was intent on gaining influence in sub-Saharan countries. The way he was intending to do this was by supplying them with medicines, particularly animal medicines.

My colleague Bryan Shand was an expert on agriculture, as I have stated, but he was also a fine businessman. It was he who came up with a clever idea to increase our sales. We used to sell big stacking drums of these medicines. When the storehouses were completely full of these drums, Bryan showed the storemen how to stack the drums on top of each other and in a quadrangle with the dimensions of a large room, thus creating another store to put further drums inside. When he was asked by management how he was able to sell so much product, his terse reply was, 'Sincerity, chief, sincerity.'

As I say, I was not truly immersed in the culture of Libya, but I knew enough to avoid standing out too obviously as some sort of colonial Brit. I never wore a suit whilst I was there; instead, I wore jeans and a leather coat, trying to look like a revolutionary. I wore my hair long too, which is something I no longer have the resources to do! Despite my attempts to blend in, however, there were still times when I felt I was in danger.

Once, I was in a hotel in Benghazi when a mob arrived outside, determined to make their anti-Western sentiments felt against us guests. The Israeli air force had shot down a Libyan plane over Egypt in February 1973 and feelings ran hot against Israel and those countries who supported the Israeli government. I deployed what had become a standard routine for such emergencies – sticking little wooden wedges under the doors so that they could not be forced open. I did not mind them attacking the hotel, but I was fearful of them setting fire to the building, I must say.

Chapter 4 *The Socialist Republics*

When I was four years old I found fishing and it has been my base ever since

Chris Tarrant

By the end of the nineteen seventies, I had been producing pretty good results in Africa and when the Chairman of Wellcome called me in to say that there was no great future, financially speaking, for the company there, I was surprised.

There was no problem in selling product in the Eastern bloc countries but getting paid did prove troublesome, for they had very little hard currency. One had to think of all sorts of ways to help customers get the necessary money for the pharmaceuticals they needed. In resolving these issues, I found that I became a very successful switch trader, probably one of the best in the business, if that is not too immodest a claim.

Wellcome had factories all over the world, for instance in India. I would go to a country which had hard currency, namely US dollars or sterling. One example was Indonesia, where there were no international restrictions on the country's banking systems. There I would meet the agent and get him to place an order for ten or twenty container loads of, say, cough medicine. He would give me a letter of credit for the value of this order and this letter of credit, or LC, as they were normally called, would be worded very specifically. There would be a stipulation that the product could be shipped from any country, not specifically from The United Kingdom. This product had to be of the highest quality, of course, and manufactured to UK standards.

I would then arrange for the shipment of medicine to be sent from Wellcome's Indian factory. The advantage here was that India had an open trading account with Russia. The USSR was supplying India with the tanks and weaponry that it required, and the Indian government was very anxious to settle the debt that they had with the USSR. Instead of monetary payment, the Russians were happy to be supplied in turn with medicines and pharmaceuticals.

They did not want Indian cough medicines however; they wanted anti-cancer drugs from Wellcome. There was a profit margin of 90% on these anti-cancer drugs, whereas the margins on the cough medicines would be only about 20-30%. I would have a million pounds worth of drugs that the Russians wanted, that had been paid for by the LC.

Switch trading meant that you switched trading at the point of origin. It was all quite legal. One might wonder how I gained this expertise in switch trading. I have to say that I found out everything I needed to know by drinking lots and lots of alcohol with traders from the Soviet bloc countries.

I also did a considerable amount of business in Hungary, where I discovered that it paid off for me to trade in produce other than pharmaceuticals. One of the big products which Wellcome was not fully involved in was insecticides. If you think of all the food grown in the world that requires potent insecticides, it is easy to see that there is a huge market. One insecticide in particular interested me.

Wellcome had been licensed by the UK government to produce pyrethroids, one of which was a substance called permethrin, a very effective insecticide. The process employed was quite clever. Put simply, scientists needed to produce an ester, which is an organic alcohol combined with an organic acid. The esterification process was comparatively simple. The Hungarians were very clever chemists and quite capable of undertaking this process, but though they could make the acid and the alcohol, they would be breaking Wellcome's patent if they combined the two to make permethrin.

I had a lightbulb moment. It was easy to make the alcohol part of the ester, but much harder to make the acid part. I said to the

Hungarian chemists, 'You make the acid, then ship it to London. You won't be breaking any patents by doing this. We will conduct the esterification process and ship the ester back to you. We will keep a high proportion of the product you make, of course.' Because the product was so high-tech, they could trade it as a valuable commodity for the hard currency they required themselves to purchase vital commodities such as oil.

I set up this arrangement and it was so profitable for the company that I was granted leave to use the chairman's aeroplane to go out to Eastern Europe to do these deals. I say the Chairman's plane, but it was actually an aircraft that belonged to McAlpine, the construction company, but licensed for the Wellcome Chairman's use. I have to confess it felt rather special driving onto the tarmac at Luton airport and flying out to Budapest by private plane.

We sent about 60% of the permethrin back to Hungary, so it was my job to find a market for the remaining 40%. Luckily, Dow Chemicals, one of the three largest chemical companies in the world, got involved and they were happy to buy all the stuff I was prepared to sell. This was a key element in the whole deal because it would have been inconvenient, pointless even, to have warehouses stacked with permethrin. These were interesting times.

My trips to Budapest were approximately once a month but I saw that there were other deals that could be done too, apart from the high value permethrin trade. It was clear that lots of low-tech commodities could also be bought and sold to generate hard currency, which was what the Hungarians needed for the purchase of Wellcome product. The glass industry in Hungary was one that was well-established and highly thought of, so it occurred to me that I could buy glassware such as retorts, test tubes, petri dishes and glass cases for science laboratories in schools, colleges and universities. It was relatively simple to obtain orders too. I would send a catalogue of the various glassware items to the purchasing arm of such institutions, and they would tick off what they wanted. My part in this process was partly as trade facilitator, but also partly technical, because I knew something about the exact specifications of the commodities that were produced in the Hungarian factories.

This enterprise was very profitable because it served as a sort of discount on the pharmaceutical product as far as the Hungarians were concerned, but it translated into hard cash for Wellcome.

It needs to be remembered that throughout the nineteen seventies and eighties Britain was at war, in a sense, with the USSR. It was the cold war, of course, but there was a good deal of suspicion, hostility and danger, even, for anyone who had to deal with the soviet bloc. I did not relish visits to Moscow, and as a consequence I tried to conduct my business in the other communist countries. As I have indicated, Budapest was one of the cities I frequented, but I also spent some time in Belgrade, in what used to be Yugoslavia. The city is known for its brutalist architecture, but it was also a fairly brutal place to be in the late seventies. Nevertheless, I preferred to be there than in Moscow.

Wellcome had agents in Yugoslavia who were sharp people. They realised the fundamentals of trading – that you have to sell something for more than it cost to produce in order to make a profit. It is surprising how few people in the world fully apprehend this. At the most basic level, people sell their labour, but not always at a price that makes it worthwhile for them to do so. I never fell into that trap.

Some of the staff I was employing in the soviet bloc countries had been marked by the British security services as persons of interest. The Chairman of Wellcome at one point said he wanted to give my name to such and such a person. That person might ask me to keep an eye on things and report back on contacts these people might be meeting, who in turn were possibly agents for the KGB.

The web of intrigue that existed at this time has been well documented by a number of novelists., such as John Le Carré and Charles Cummings, and there have been numerous films about spies and the people caught up in dubious activities in these nervous days. One such man was Greville Wynne, an engineer and businessman famous in the nineteen sixties for his liaison with the MI6 recruit Oleg Penkovsky. He was, in fact, recently portrayed on film by Benedict Cumberbatch, which I thought was excellent casting, because of the remarkable physical likeness between the two men. Wynne was instrumental in obtaining information from his Russian contact that was crucial to the West during the Cuban missile crisis. I did not want to end up like Wynne in Lubyanka prison, however, so I decided, wisely I think, that I would only deal with the chairman of Wellcome and with MI5 and MI6. There was no way of knowing who amongst my Wellcome colleagues might have been compromised and no way of knowing who amongst the British secret service was a double agent.

I mentioned earlier that the chairman of Wellcome had a secretary who reminded me of Miss Moneypenny, and it may sound here like I fancied myself a sort of James Bond, talking to M, but this was by no means the case. I was a businessman and never equipped for or desirous of, any role in espionage. I have been inside Thames House, but it seemed to me like any normal civil service building. Much scarier was the business of going thorough Moscow Airport. You would hand your passport over to a Russian official and then wait for perhaps an hour or longer before it was handed back, all the while aware of the suspicious and threatening eyes on you.

On these trips to Moscow, I stayed in hotels where I am sure that my room was bugged, and it is more than possible that someone may have been listening in to my telephone calls when I was back in England too. Sometimes at home, after I had gone to bed, I would get a call from overseas. These calls were, of course, purely business related and not exceptional, because of the different time zones involved. I would deliberately not replace the receiver, to check if anyone was sitting in a room somewhere in some nondescript building listening. Sometimes I heard a voice on the line reciting code numbers and so forth. It all sounds very amateurish to me now, and it was definitely not foreign agents who were interested in my conversations.

I used to leave Moscow on a four o'clock flight on Friday afternoon on a British airways flight, and when we had taken off there would be a tremendous cheer from all the Brits who had been working in the city that week. A cheer of joy that we were returning home, but also, I suspect, a cheer of relief that we had yet again managed to escape a regime that was deeply suspicious of us

Westerners.

In Yugoslavia I used to stay in Belgrade, which was much less threatening than Moscow. I also spent time in Leipzig, but the city was a fairly dismal place after the East German government had moved the creative industries elsewhere and created a heavy industry miasma over everything. Of course, the German Democratic Republic as a whole was no bundle of fun during the Cold War. On the other hand, I enjoyed my trips to Poland because the Poles were trustworthy, and in my opinion good people. I frequented Czechoslovakia too. Bratislava was interesting and Prague was a genuinely nice place, especially the impressive central Wenceslas Square where I would stay. I appreciated the glorious old Bohemian feel of this city. I did little sightseeing, however, because most of my time would be spent talking to international trade organisations whose representatives would attend these never-ending trade fairs and expos.

Some of the people that Wellcome wanted to influence were Director-Generals of state research organisations. At that time, the British government was perhaps working to try and destabilise foreign institutions. Names would be picked out for me, and I had to make approaches to such people. It is much easier to buy than to sell, so I would initiate contact by asking them what I could buy from them. Then I would mention that there was a trade fair coming up in, say, San Francisco.

'Are you planning to go there?' I would ask disingenuously. To gain their trust and respect I would then assure them that I could get them a ticket for the fair. I would flatter these men by stressing that everyone would be extremely interested in their expert views on such and such a matter. Two things were happening here. Anybody in the socialist republics, even the Director-General of an establishment, would have to have the permission of his local branch of the communist party to go to such an event. They could either say yes or no.

If they said yes, the man or woman would go to San Francisco and inevitably be exposed to the fact that soviet propaganda about how advanced their technology was compared to that of the West was simply untrue. If they said no, the scientist would be aggrieved about his or her own political bosses, who were not allowing him or her to demonstrate their expertise and intellect, because clearly they were regarded as a person of international renown. This in contrast to the members of the local political party, who in all likelihood were uneducated people in menial jobs. Either way, the West gained a psychological advantage. It was Wellcome who provided the budget for this international travel and attendance at trade fairs, but it may well have been our own government which was the instigating force behind this destabilising policy. I was not aware then of the genesis of such schemes and I do not wish to hypothesise about it at this stage, even though all these shenanigans took place fifty years ago.

I was Marketing Manager, Socialist Republics, but I also had another responsibility in the field of technology transfer. The science in most of the socialist countries was not first rate, apart from in Hungary, where the scientists were excellent, as I have pointed out. They were producing a drug called trimethoprim, but there was a problem because it transpired that they had copied a process which Wellcome had patented. I was obliged to go and talk to the scientists at the company that was making this drug, because we felt that they were breaking the patent.

The Hungarians claimed that they had introduced an aniline derivative in their own synthesis, and it was merely a coincidence that this step in the process was the same step as that made by Wellcome. Therefore, they said, they had not broken the patent. These were the early days of mass spectrometry, and I spent a lot of time with some of the Wellcome chemists, who were leading people in their field, testing their claim. With our advanced kit we were able to detect traces of an anilino in the trimethoprim, and these trace amounts acted almost as a fingerprint. Science is sometimes like detective work! We were able to prove that the Hungarian scientists had broken patent law.

They were basically good people, so I said that we had no need to go to international court. 'You won't stand a chance,' I said, 'because these are the indisputable traces.' Then I offered them a way out. 'How do we square this?' I said. 'I want to do business with you. I don't want to give money to lawyers.'

I offered them a deal. 'Imagine a pot,' I said, 'and think of it as a large pot that can be filled with money. For everything you buy from me I will put 10% of that payment in the pot. For anything I buy from you, I want 10% of that payment to go in the pot as well. When the pot is full, we are even. Your job is to fill that pot as quickly as you possibly can. Preferably while I am still in this job.' Since no one else in the Wellcome sales team understood the chemistry, I was in a unique position. Hence I contrived to form a very special relationship with these Hungarian scientists, and a relationship that was mutually beneficial.

I was also fortunate to have a man called Laslo Naj on my side. Laslo was the EC patent examiner and Brussels bureaucrat. He was a Hungarian émigré who was not attuned to the Hungarian government. His influence is further evidence that even such a pure field as pharmaceuticals was not able to resist political pressure. But, above all, work in this field was heavily reliant on personal relationships. I would offer my trust to people, and they would trust me. Or perhaps the opposite.

Chapter 5 *Smith, Kline and French*

Fishing is about the unexpected. You sit there waiting for one thing and then something totally different comes along

Jeremy Wade

I left Wellcome in 1982 to join Smith, Kline and French. I had, of course, been running Agropharm concurrently and I continued to do so as I worked for the new company, but I only worked for the company for a relatively short time, for reasons I will make apparent presently.

While I was working at Agropharm I knew that the Americans were buying a lot of worming material for the feed lots for the cattle industry. The valuable stuff was phenothiazine, which I bought off spec from Russia. The purity was good, but the particle size rendered it useless, so that was when I contacted someone in Huddersfield who had the equipment to grind it down so that it could be used as the cattle vermicide. Just the one shipment yielded £500,000 but chemical trading is so incestuous that you can only pull off a deal like that only once. Therefore, I now had to seek other opportunities.

But I should relate something about my time at Smith, Kline and French. One of the most important drugs developed by my new company was Tagamet, the brand name given to cimetidine, a highly effective treatment for ulcers. Even up till the late nineteen seventies peptic ulcers could prove life-threatening, but the research done by a small group of brilliant scientists at Smith, Kline and French created one of the first treatments to be formulated from logical principles, rather than experimentation with organic material. James

Black led this work. Traditionally, a new drug's development would often depend on the fortuitous discovery of a plant or microbial extract that showed some of the required biological activity. Using that first extract as a lead, many similar compounds would be made and tested for pharmacological effectiveness. In many cases, the researchers did not know how the drug worked, so finding an optimal compound was difficult. The development of cimetidine was radically different, in that it involved the identification of a molecule which would compete with histamine and prevent acids combining with a receptor in the stomach lining, the root cause of the painful effect of stomach ulcers. I am proud to say that one of the key figures in this ground-breaking work was a fellow Welshman, Graham Durant, who worked under James Black.

Though I was at Smith, Kline and French for only a short period of time, about eighteen months, lots of interesting things happened. One of these involved Tagamet.

Tagamet was a crucial drug for gastric bleeding, ulcer treatment and so forth. Now, as it was so effective, it was globally very profitable for the company. Unfortunately, it is inevitable that whenever there is a product that can earn so much, counterfeiters quickly appear on the scene. So it proved in Nigeria. Smith, Kline and French devoted a huge amount of time and money trying to stamp out this illegal activity but for a while were unsuccessful. What was at stake was not just profit, of course. People could, and did, die of gastric bleeding. Ultimately the American executives decided to take radical steps. They hired a man called Brushweiler, an ex-Mossad agent, to look into the matter.

Brushweiler had good contacts at Interpol but not so many in Africa. Therefore, it was my role to look after him in Nigeria and provide him with all the help he needed. When he flew in, I picked him up at the airport and we went to the American embassy in Lagos, where he collected his gun and 'shock stick' or taser. He was not particularly prepossessing to look at; he was slight balding fellow, but I could tell he was not a man to be trifled with even before he told me of his exploits as a pilot in the Arab Israeli Six Day War.

What we discovered was that the counterfeit stuff was being

made in Hong Kong. The gang running the scheme had tableting machines that were kept in containers in the backs of lorries; hence their operation was mobile. Nobody was ever able to raid some isolated building on a trading estate, as we see in movies and TV shows where the police have detected an illegal drug making operation.

The fake tablets were good fakes, but I was experienced enough to be able to look at them and see that they were not the real thing. I did not even need to test the constituents, because it was apparent to me that they were mere placebos, even from just the surface of the tablets.

What Brushweiler and I came up with was quite a clever strategy. We concluded that we needed to trace our way down the value chain. As you go down the value chain you get closer to the importer. If, for instance, Smith, Kline and French were selling Tagamet for a pound, everybody else would want to sell it cheaper. When you got down to fifty pence you were close to the importer. So, by looking at the pharmacies' invoices and seeing what they were paying their suppliers, you could tell who might be the likely importer. A series of phone taps was set up too.

Once we got the passport number of this person, we could track his movements. It is hard to believe now but I recall being in the American embassy when I saw a stream of messages several feet long pouring forth from the telex machine. They indicated every hotel this man had stayed in, every flight he had been on. He would fly with British Caledonian Airways to London every Monday, then fly British Airways to Hong Kong. There he would pick up his contraband, fly back to Paris. From there he would fly to Benin, which we knew then as Dahomey of course. He would load the car he kept here with the drugs and drive up the creeks to a place called Badagri. He would meet agents there who took the material from him. It would only be a couple of suitcases, but the contents would be worth a great deal of money. He was a slippery customer and also a dangerous man.

This detective work was not something that I felt I could get too involved in, because there was potential for a lot of violence.

Brushweiler had no such compunctions, however. He was in his element in fact. I suppose I should have realised this from the outset, when he saw fit to arm himself with a pistol and a taser. He was not a direct employee of Smith, Kline and French, or indeed any of the big pharmaceutical companies. He was a freelancer who worked for a number of agencies. I gathered that he had based himself in Monte Carlo in order to be close to Northern Italy, where he was able to keep an eye on anti-American Mafia activity.

My role was to take the counterfeit material, seal it up and post it off to Smith, Kline and French's laboratory in Geneva and also to the Nigerian authority's laboratory. After testing, the Nigerians claimed that the tablets contained 100% of the claimed active constituents; the lab in Geneva, however, found that there was no trace of any active constituent. It transpired that the importer was splitting his profits with the Northern People's Party, hence no prosecution ever took place. I am sorry to say this was just one example of the corruption that was rife throughout the country at that time.

The reason men like me were employed by Big Pharma was to try and counteract this institutional corruption. The modus operandi was for us to go into a shop and pick up what was being sold as Tagamet. If I put it down again right side up it was what we were looking for, the corrupt material. If it was kosher, I would put it back down the other way.

What ensued thereafter was proof of a level of institutional violence that I could not stomach. Anybody with counterfeit material would be arrested and taken to a police cell. There they would be beaten across the buttocks and the back with a 4"x2" piece of wood. I knew that my Israeli colleague was not a man I could easily trust. I remember going to the yacht club in Lagos and catching part of a conversation he was having with some fellow Israelis. He was expounding on his theory that his country had grown and would need to expand its borders by laying claim to other countries' territory. It is a strange fact, but some of the Europeans who joined the exodus to the new state of Israel to escape the fascist backgrounds of their native Germany and Austria in 1948 proved to be the most fervent in terms of their aggressive attitude to their neighbours. Brushweiler was Austrian by birth.

I said nothing about these expansionist desires, but I told Brushweiler the company was not paying me enough for me to have my sense of right and wrong challenged so emphatically by the savage methods employed by him and his police friends. It was at about this time that I decided I should give up my job with Smith, Kline and French and leave Nigeria.

Smith, Kline and French was, in my opinion, very badly run, at least in Nigeria. They were wary of deploying Americans in country because of the prevalence of Anti-American feeling and activities, so they put two young Irish accountants in charge of the business. These lads were naïve, to say the least. They employed the wrong people; they bribed the wrong people and therefore did not protect the company adequately. When I took over, the indebtedness of the Nigerian company to its parent company in America was in excess of £5 million. As much as £3 million of this was written off as bad debt. The problem was that they had put the money in the central bank with inadequate documentation, so that bank could not give witness to the deposits. Effectively, the money was locked away and unusable.

It was my job to unjam this situation, and I knew that I could, though obviously I hoped for some sort of flexible remuneration for my efforts. Fortunately, there was a man in Nigeria who once ran Standard Bank. Patently he knew some of the Central Bank people and he and I agreed that if he could use his sources to release the moneys locked up, we could solve my employer's problem. By a simple twist of fate, as Bob Dylan would put it, he was a Welshman from North Wales. Stranger still, he hailed from Corwen, the village where I had met my wife. He had no intentions of returning to his homeland, however, because he married a Yoruba woman and learned to speak the Yoruba language. As a result, he was equipped to deal with Nigerians very well. How he got to be called 'Chief' by his Nigerian friends and colleagues is an interesting little tale. As a young man he was living somewhere out in the backwaters and these places can be very violent. The chief of his village nearby was under threat, and he offered this chief refuge in his home. His reward was the honorary title of Chief himself.

As I mentioned, I made it clear to my superiors that I had to go, but the circumstances of my departure were fairly dramatic. More of this in a moment. I had done all I could for the company, though there were still some bits and pieces that needed to be tidied up. I suggested a successor and he was offered the job. This man had worked with me in Wellcome, and he was a good man.

One piece of advice I offered him when he arrived to take up his position was to travel everywhere by taxi. There was a company car, a lovely Mercedes 300, but there was a serious danger of being targeted by criminal elements if he allowed himself to be driven around in such a conspicuous vehicle. There was, I felt, an accountant in the company who had been taking money from Smith, Kline and French's debtors, in order for him to write off their debts. These people were traders who were incensed when they were told that their debts were not to be written off after all. I am afraid to say that it was likely that their solution to a problem might well be to get rid of the person causing the problem. Accordingly, I had been very concerned about my personal safety and had taken a series of counter measures. I stayed in different hotels, turned up for work at different times, and, as I say, used taxis for transportation. It transpired that my fears were not unfounded. Not long after I left Nigeria, I heard that the Mercedes had been shot at. A motorbike drew up alongside the Mercedes and the pillion passenger fired several rounds from an Israeli manufactured Uzi machine gun through the windows. My successor escaped unhurt, but his marketing manager was hit and had to be taken to hospital by an urgent medical evacuation.

The circumstance of my leaving Nigeria and Smith, Kline and French were, as I say dramatic. I was medically evacuated myself, in a sense. I happened like this: one evening I was invited to a party because I was regarded as someone who was useful in networking. I suppose you would say, in today's parlance, I was an 'influencer.' When I got home from the engagement that night, I felt very unwell. I had a terrible fever, and I was sweating so much that Ann had to help me take the mattress, which was soaked through, out onto the balcony to try and dry it. I thought I had malaria but was also concerned that it might be something worse than that, like Lassa fever. I went to the doctor, but he was not able to do much for me. I decided I needed to get back to Britain. Of course, one was not supposed to travel with the sort of high temperature that I had. Despite this, I managed to talk my way onto a flight home.

Once on the plane and out of Nigerian airspace I got a message to the pilot requesting that an ambulance be ready at Heathrow to take me to hospital. Furthermore, I asked for someone from Smith, Kline and French to meet me at the airport. I was taken straight from the airport to the London Hospital for Tropical Diseases. What I was suffering from was diagnosed as 'pyrexia of unknown origin.' It was almost certainly a virus, but the medics' inability to be more specific about the nature of my infection was, to say the least, troubling.

Our daughter Bryony was not involved in any of this drama because she was at school in Berkhamsted. This school, like the school she subsequently attended in Brecon, was founded in the sixteenth century. The sixteenth century historian William Camden noted that the school building was 'the only structure in Berkhamsted worth a second glance'. We did not send her to the school purely for the aesthetic qualities of its buildings, of course. Ann, however, was still out in Nigeria with our young son Hefin. Needless to say, she was resourceful enough to be able to make good her own departure with all due haste.

I got back to Britain and my own company, Agropharm, with a few shekels (to reprise my earlier Israeli theme). This agricultural products business was a thriving concern, but I had ambitions to build our own pharmaceutical company. Because I had left Smith, Kline and French of my own accord I did not receive a bumper pay-off. Having said that, I had amassed a small pot of cash through being given a percentage of the moneys I had saved the company. Also, I had the foresight to bank it safely in Swiss accounts. Also, in 1976 I had established Penn Pharmaceuticals in my Welsh base at Tredegar.

Bryan Shand and I had decided that we wanted to branch out from agricultural products and get into the pharmaceutical business, where the profit margins were much better. We knew it was far too expensive, in terms of both real estate and labour costs, to set anything up in the home counties, and as a result we decided to come to Wales. We knew that we could rent a site from The Welsh Development Agency. We found a ten-acre site in Tredegar. It had just one building, or shed, as I like to think of it now, but it was quite large. Ten thousand square feet, in fact. From this point on, as a piece of inverted snobbery, I guess, I called myself 'The Man in the Shed in Tredegar'

The company was named Penn Pharmaceuticals, the name deriving from the village near High Wycombe where we had started Agropharm. I like the name not merely because it was this Buckinghamshire village where my business enterprises began, but also because of its Welsh association. It is thought by some that the name derives from the Welsh word *pen,* or head, since the village is situated at the head of a piece of woodland. There are others who dispute this theory, claiming the village was named after William Penn, whose family hailed from Buckinghamshire and Wiltshire. Penn is famous, needless to say, because he was one of the first and most important Quakers to emigrate to America. He founded the state of Pennsylvania and became Governor of that state. Also, I think interestingly, he was the first person to argue for a United States of Europe. He did so a couple of hundred years before the actual formation of the European Union.

Setting up Penn Pharmaceuticals in Wales was a venture that was not without its risks, plainly, and felt I could not up sticks straight away and leave Hertfordshire. Thus, I used to have to travel from Leighton Buzzard to Tredegar nearly every day, which was very wearing.

I knew little about building pharmaceutical facilities, but I did know enough people who had expertise in this regard. We were fortunate in our timing because the pharmaceutical industry in the UK was contracting and there was a lot of good plant and machinery available second-hand. What we needed was mixers and blenders and tableting machines and we were able to acquire such items relatively inexpensively. Accordingly, we gradually built up a going concern.

It was hard to break into the industry, but we managed it. The industry was making drugs which would fulfil 98% of the needs of customers, but not 100%. Fortunately, there was legislation which allowed companies to make so-called 'specials' or unlicensed products. Normally such medicines are made in the public sector, by hospitals for example. Frequently, sad to say, they did not make a great job of manufacturing them, so I thought that I could offer something that was an improved version of these 'specials'.

As unlicensed products they could not be claimed to be totally effective in the treatment of conditions, but we could claim that our version contained all the right chemical components. We were hence able to sell to hospitals.

In course of time, we realised that there was a lot of money to be made in the business of clinical trials. These trials are extensive and normally take a long time, but I thought the process could be speeded up. The way that trials for a vaccination for Covid-19 were conducted in record time is a recent remarkable demonstration of how rapidly it can be done.

Instead of making a thousand tablets for hospitals I thought I could make ten thousand tablets for clinical studies. You had to make both the active drug and the placebo so that they appeared identical, in order that no one would know which treatment they were receiving. I became very effective in making tablets and capsules of both the active drug and the placebo. Naturally, a lot of meticulous testing had to take place, but we had the expertise and the will to undertake the work speedily. I am proud to say that Penn became a principal manufacturer of drugs for clinical trials in the United Kingdom. This is quite an achievement when you consider that Glaxo, for example, were a pharmaceutical business with immense resources to conduct such trials. What is true, though, is that their most able pharmacists engaged in other work. Usually, it was some of the lowlier pharmacists who worked on clinical trials.

If you have a twenty-year patent and you waste twelve years dithering you only have eight years to commercialise your product. What I was offering was a very valuable service, because although we did not manufacture the active ingredients, we had all the methodology for the analytical work and testing. We made the drugs available for trials much faster than big pharma. Our chemists dealt with a new product every month; companies like Glaxo were perhaps only testing a new product every year. In other words, we were much slicker in what we did.

We did not have deals with all the big pharma companies, so I needed to explore opportunities on a global scale. I knew that Japan had a very large pharmaceutical industry, second only to The United States, and I took a rather bold step and cold-called a number of firms there. They could not believe what I was telling them in terms of our time compression for development of drugs. They were more than happy to use us to prepare products for clinical testing in the United Kingdom. This in turn enabled them to access the British sales markets.

As the company grew and it became clear that it was going to be a success, I realised that I could not continue commuting from Leighton Buzzard to Tredegar. Accordingly, Ann and I began the search for a new home. It was important to move at this time because my daughter Bryony had just finished her GCSEs and we wanted to settle somewhere where she could embark upon her 'A' level studies without them being interrupted mid-term. It was 1989 when we found my present house. I will say a little more about the house later because it has an interesting history.

It was also a suitable time to look for a permanent home in Wales because my son Hefin was ten years old, and I knew it would be only fair for him to have a settled home until he was old enough to go to university. He is a very bright young man, and he was offered a place at Christ College, starting a year early. Ann decided it would be better for him to go to a local school, however, so he was sent to a small primary school in nearby Cradoc, so that he could integrate with children from the neighbourhood before moving up to secondary school. Therefore, he joined his sister at Christ College a year later. As far as the children's education was concerned, it was a wise choice to move to our home near Brecon. The school is one of the oldest and most successful independent schools in the United Kingdom and, because there are only 350 pupils, it boasts an enviable staff to student ratio as well as first rate teaching.

Though I was still a sleeping partner with my good friend Bryan Shand in our Agropharm enterprise, I was in charge of Penn Pharmaceuticals, with Bryan as my sleeping partner The company was turning over in excess of £12 million per annum, which yielded quite a healthy profit, and the future was looking good. I knew there was quite some value in the company, but I was growing tired of the grind and stress of never having sufficient capital. I was always looking for funds because of the need to replace machinery etcetera I was keen to start other ventures and get back into purer scientific work in the field of pharmaceutical research. We decided to sell Penn in 1999 and I arranged a management buy-out. It made sense to convert the obvious asset I had into cash. Bryan and I shared the money we received from the sale equally because we had a *pareil partout* agreement regarding the ownership of Agropharm and Penn. It was not until 2016 that Bryan and I agreed to sell Agropharm.

I had lots of ideas about the pharmaceutical industry, for instance to get into freeze-drying. I knew how the process worked, but the machinery involved could cost as much as two million pounds. I was not prepared to stake that sort of money. Instead, with the capital I raised from this sale I was able to set up several companies. I will say more about these ventures presently.

Chapter 6 *Public Service*

Fishing is a hard job. You have to be wise and smart. And quick
Mariano Rivera

As I mentioned, I was tired of the quotidian grind at Penn, and I was glad that the management there were keen to buy me out. I saw this move as an opportunity for me to get involved more in the public sector. I considered I could play some part in industrial policy making, but also in other sectors, such as the media and the environment. My first opportunity arrived in 2000 when I was asked to chair the Welsh Development Agency.

Technically, I was interviewed for the post of WDA chairman, but the process was in truth more a series of informal conversations with Rhodri Morgan, Welsh First Minister. I did continue in post for three and a half years, but I have to confess that work at the WDA was very time consuming and often extremely frustrating. One of the main aspects of my role was to meet all sorts of potential investors in Wales and do a certain amount of glad handing.

Once again, however, I found I was faced with incompetence. In particular I had a troublesome relationship with Graham Hawker, the Chief Executive of WDA. He had previously been CEO of The Welsh Water Authority. To be frank about these matters, he had bought a power company and borrowed a lot of money to finance the purchase. He thought he was the greatest finance expert in the world, but he certainly was not. He reckoned he could undermine me, as Chairman, by forging relationships with the senior Welsh politicians, none of whom was particularly au fait with the important work of the WDA. He clearly befriended these figures because he had ambitions to be chairman himself. One needs to understand the relative status of the two positions: I ran board meetings and formulated policy, whereas the Chief Executive operated the day-to-day business of the agency. It may seem churlish of me to take objection to the man in the way I am indicating, but there was something about him that rankled with me. I should perhaps quote here the English satirical poet Tom Brown. It was he who was ordered to translate an epigram by the Latin poet Martial by his Dean at university, Dr John Fell. Martial had written that he did not like a chap called Sabidias, but he did not know quite why. Brown promptly penned the lines:

I do not like thee, Dr Fell.
The reason why – I cannot tell:
But this I know, and know full well,
I do not like thee, Dr Fell.

Fortunately for me, I had Graham Hawker's card marked. The former Chairman of Hyder, the privatised former Welsh Water Authority, was a man called John Elfed Jones, who was from North Wales, like me, and he was an old friend of mine. He was a fervent supporter of Welsh language and culture (his autobiography was in Welsh), and he gained some notoriety in the early 2000s for his comments likening the influx of non-Welsh speaking outsiders into the country to 'human foot and mouth disease.' To me, he was a trusted associate and wise man who enjoyed fishing, I would say, almost as much as me. He furnished me with details about Hawker's strengths and weaknesses at Welsh water and I made it clear that no mistakes were to occur under my watch at the WDA.

Hawker eventually had to resign when Rhodri Morgan announced that he intended to close down the agency and incorporate its work into the civil service. For once, I was in agreement with Graham Hawker about this piece of political short-sightedness. As I told a committee of MPs in 2011: 'You need to be fleet of foot and you do not get fleet of foot in the civil service. The private sector is only interested with outcomes, whereas the public sector is mainly interested in process.'

The process of getting approval for projects was very complex and difficult. It was a problem trying to get people to see the relative short term, middle term and long-term advantages of any particular bid. Leads came in a variety of ways from overseas and from England. We would try and persuade companies that we would do our best to smooth the road for them, but it was frustrating when politicians muscled in and attempted to grab all the credit for any successes.

An example of one of the avenues that the WDA sought to pursue, which would have been of massive benefit to people in Wales in terms of employment opportunities, came in the shape of the giant Korean electronics firm LG. Negotiations were put in place to encourage and help the company develop their plant in Newport, but politics got in the way and the Koreans decided to relocate to Kirkcaldy, which of course was future Prime Minister Gordon Brown's constituency. Sadly, so much time was taken up over political wrangling that LG aborted the whole project and concentrated European production in Germany instead. Looking back now on those days at the WDA I see that there was definitely a firefighting-cum-ambulance side to my role, chiefly because of the constant interference by certain politicians intent on securing their own short-term advantage.

Nevertheless, there were successes during my time at the WDA. Inward investment increased quite dramatically. It was vital to encourage the growth of new industries and diversify from coal and steel after the decline of the heavy industry which had (literally) fuelled the Welsh economy for so long. In the first twenty years of its existence the WDA had helped reduce unemployment in Wales by 9.3%, a figure only marginally inferior to the 9.4% reduction in the Northwest of England. During its active years, the WDA injected roughly £12bn of inward investment into Wales and created hundreds of jobs. It was not just the influx of new firms that was significant either, for the presence of manufacturing companies obviously helped build the supply chain in Wales too.

Several years after I left the WDA there was something of an expenses scandal involving my time as chairman. *Wales Online* published an article in 2009 claiming that I had abused expense allowances whilst investigating the abuse of expenses by Welsh Assembly members. I think the circular nature of this claim is almost amusing, but the so-called facts do not bear much scrutiny.

This is what happened. I chaired an independent panel of four people, including former Plaid Cymru president Dafydd Wigley, to look into the expenses being claimed by Assembly members. We discovered that some of these politicians were claiming rents paid on second homes in Cardiff, despite the fact that they represented constituencies within easy commuting distance from the city. We also suspected that cohabiting AMs were doubling up on their expense claims. Furthermore, nearly a third of the AMs were employing close family members as staff, often without appropriate selection criteria.

I was asked to conduct a review of these matters because there was a sense that the systems in use for checking expense abuse were not exactly robust. Also, media scrutiny is very different in England and Wales. *The Western Mail* is not *The Daily Mail*. The inquiry discovered that AMs were claiming for expensive furniture and large screen TVs for their second homes in Cardiff. It is true that no AM actually claimed for the cost of erecting a duck house on an island in his garden pond but the Westminster MPs expense claim scandal definitely informed concerns in Wales about how public money was being spent.

Although all four parties at the National Assembly unanimously accepted the set of recommendations made by the independent panel, a number of AMs took offence at the tone of some of my remarks. That august organ *The Western Mail* quoted me on the day the report was released, saying something about the "lax" arrangements relating to AMs' expenses. I had said they had been a scandal waiting to happen. I can be rather forthright at times, I admit. When interviewed by one of their journalists I said, 'It's like sending kids into the sweet shop with the shelves knee-high off the ground. They were told to help themselves – and they did.' I went on to declare that anything that had 'Assembly' attached to it was tax-free. So not only were they getting something worth £500, but they were also

76

getting something worth £800.

My own expenses were not for a second home or to provide a salary for my wife or children. They mainly comprised the cost of travel and accommodation on foreign trips, plus hospitality costs abroad and within the UK. In my time as Chairman of the WDA I sometimes had to undertake long haul trips to China, Singapore, Australia and the USA, and I frequently had to travel within Europe to meet with businessmen and potential investors. The cost of these trips, including the costs incurred by the people who went with me, was met from my expense account. I did not travel in cattle class, and neither did those who had to accompany me. Not only was first class travel the most appropriate means for someone in the prominent public position I held, but also the opportunity to work whilst in transit was a vital aspect. There may have been AMs, who do not normally travel first class, who were a tad envious of this arrangement, but if they were ministers, they enjoyed the same privilege. To say that I spent in excess of £30,000 in over four years might suggest a life of luxury, but in fact it amounts to perhaps ten trips per year, all of them essential in trying to execute my responsibilities in encouraging economic development in Wales. The same goes for my overseas accommodation costs, which actually came to less than a hundred pounds per night. Perhaps the *Wales Online* journalist responsible for this muckraking expected me to stay in some YMCA when I went to America, but my youth hostelling days were well over by this time. It must be borne in mind too that I did not decide where I went when I made overseas trips; such matters were in the purview of the overseas branch of the WDA.

The *Wales Online* article documents claims made for taxi fares and the sum it cites is £6,000. I have to say this in no way reflects the use I made of taxis; rather it reflects the claims that were made by any number of officials for journeys they may have made on business trips that I sanctioned. They simply claimed against my expense account. The figure quoted for refreshments, meals etc was £4,300, which seems like a large amount, but this sum covered a period of over four years. It is actually equivalent to an expenditure of £20 per week. Hardly a king's ransom. But it would be egregious to account for the accusations made by Wales Online one by one. Suffice it to say I documented all expenses accurately and fairly and have no regrets. The salary I received was not excessive and the benefits the WDA brought to the Welsh economy were significant.

I was always attracted to the BBC because of the sheer talent of so many of its staff, so I was delighted to join the Board of Governors when I was appointed Chairman of the Welsh Broadcasting Council in 1996. The work basically meant looking after London interests in Wales and Welsh interests in London. This dual role was very important because, though you would not think it, not everybody was pulling in the same direction. Indeed, they were not always pulling on the same rope. This was because there were so many different agendas at board level.

We had a board meeting in London once a month where we sat down with senior BBC staff and kicked around the complaints, threats and comments made about BBC productions and BBC policies. Though I had held several senior positions in my work as a pharmacist and businessman and had had to deal with all sorts of powerful people in a wide range of situations at home and abroad, I found I still had a lot to learn about the politics of public institutions. And I did I learn a great deal during these board meetings.

Our role was to establish policy and to ensure that policy was being enacted. There were issues over language, types of programming, questions of excessive violence in drama and news coverage, to name just a few of the relevant areas. Cultural issues such as diversity were also addressed. The word 'diversity' these days invariably adumbrates notions of age, ethnicity, gender, sexuality and disability, but there were and are other pertinent notions, such as the cultural differences that exist between North Wales and South Wales in terms of norms and values. I was brought up as a Welsh speaker in a small village in North Wales and educated in a large English-speaking city in South Wales, so I was well aware of the cultural differences of both language and community structure.

I am a proud Welshman and Welsh speaker, but I am also a pragmatic soul. Though I plainly want Welsh to survive and thrive as a language you just have to accept that English is the principal language of public discourse. I do, of course, recognise that there is clearly a place for the Welsh language in the arts. A more radical view of these matters was proposed by one organisation that would consistently lobby the BBC. *Cymdeithas Yr Iaith*, which translates as The Welsh Language Society, strongly urged public bodies to pay greater heed to Welsh language and culture. I say 'urged' but I could say 'pestered'. They would regularly question why the BBC ran one series rather than another series more sympathetic to the unique Welsh culture, for example.

The dual role of the BBC in Wales was to represent itself in Welsh events such as the National Eisteddfod, and to represent Welsh interests in its news coverage and other programming. If someone wrote an article or made a statement which was not reflective of the strong feelings of such activists, a fire would be lit that we had to put out. I use the word 'fire' figuratively of course, but it is not an inappropriate term, considering the activities of another Welsh group of activists, *Meibion Glyndwr*, in the nineteen eighties and nineties.

I held my position as BBC governor concurrently with my role as chairman of the WDA. These two positions were, of course two of the most powerful in Wales. Certain Labour politicians held strong views about this situation. Also, I do not think it is unfair to suspect that they may have held ambitions to promote friends and allies to power. Despite these tensions I was at the BBC for six years. And I enjoyed the discussions we held over programming at our board meetings. The really big issues, however, inevitably concerned politics, rather than how much comedy, how much drama, how many soap operas or reality shows were being aired.

The BBC is often viewed as having slightly left-wing bias, which to me is no bad thing. In fact, it delights me. There are, of course, those who deplore what they see as the right wing tendences of the institution. If some people are complaining about the company being too left-wing and some people are complaining about it being too right-wing, it makes sense to me to think that the BBC has got it about right.

Hugely controversial were such things as the coverage of Princess Diana's death. There was what I consider to be mass hysteria in the country over the death of someone who had been a very visible public figure but was now essentially a private citizen. The Princess was evidently a personable young woman with some excellent qualities, though I do not think it is too controversial to claim great intellect was not one of them, yet the grief expressed by a huge portion of the populace was remarkable. We had to be aware that the BBC needed to select a representative sample of the people's points of view and avoid too much in the way of controversial views. Viewers pay for their television licence and have entitlements.

In my own view the reality of the tragedy was that Diana was too naïve to comprehend that the security offered her by Mohamed Al-Fayed's people was nothing like the security she had been afforded by the British security services. This was not a view which was represented in BBC features, however, because there was a fixation at Broadcasting House about avoiding criticism from the tabloid press, I remember on one occasion, when we were yet again under attack for some perceived infraction, a female civil servant, a woman with an IQ of about 80 on a hot day, saying to Christopher Bland, the Chairman of the BBC while I was there, 'Christopher, have you seen the red tops today?'

Bland was a robust character, with a rather chauvinistic tendency to give short shrift to female colleagues, and he replied in his gruff but educated voice, 'Of course I f***ing have!' The note of something like panic in the woman's voice and the note of ire in Bland's response, I think, show how aware we were at the BBC of the power and hostility of the popular press.

I related earlier that I was fond of music in my youth. My tastes were always eclectic, but I enjoyed classical music more at this stage in my life. One of my own fixations was the BBC National Orchestra of Wales, and its continued welfare. It was partially funded by the Welsh Assembly, but it also received funding from the BBC. It had grown during the nineteen eighties to a full symphonic complement of eighty-eight players, but cuts were an inevitable threat on the horizon. The number of musicians was eventually reduced in 2014, a cut which was accompanied by a number of redundancies for staff in administration and management.

Another hobby horse of mine was serious drama. It was always a big disappointment to me that we did not have a Welsh drama series. I fought hard to get this, and I am glad to see now that some superior dramas in my native language have at last been televised and received recognition. In addition, there is now a healthy production line in terms of dramas in English filmed in Wales, using Welsh talent.

A great mistake in Wales was the process of commissioning of Welsh dramas. In this respect S4C did not do us many favours. They tended to commission programmes from small production companies, but in doing so they were carving a small cake into very small, and thus unviable, pieces. This was a mistake. I became increasingly aware of this flaw when I joined the board of S4C after I had left the BBC.

Before I describe that experience though I should say something about the crises that afflicted the BBC, both before I joined the board of governors and after I relinquished that role. The corporation had always enjoyed a somewhat troublesome relationship with the government, and with those organs of the print media antagonistic to its independence and putative neutrality. Obviously, I am mainly talking about the 'red tops' but there was criticism from the broadsheet press too.

Before my time there had been the controversial sacking of Director-general Alasdair Milne by Duke Hussey, a Thatcher appointee as Chair of the Governing Body. Many saw Hussey as a hatchet man put in place to get rid of a critic of Margaret Thatcher. Hussey was not just a political puppet either; he had strong royal connections through his marriage to the one of the Queen's 'women of the bedchamber'. This is not as salacious as it sounds; it is a term similar to 'Lady-in-waiting'. Certainly anyway, the board was stacked with pro-Conservative members, including William Rees-Mogg, who had stood twice as a prospective Tory MP, and whose son and daughter became respectively MP and MEP as Conservatives. Also, there were some serious donors to the Tory party. In his television series *Days That Shook the BBC* in 2022, David Dimbleby did an excellent analysis of the corporation's relationship with the great estates of government and monarchy. In accordance with his BBC even-handedness, he talked about the row he had had himself with former Labour Prime Minister Harold Wilson, so there is no issue of left- or right-wing bias.

Yet to emerge was the controversy over the Martin Bashir interview with Princess Diana. Prince William, for one, criticised the BBC heavily over his mother's interview with Bashir. Still more recently there was a degree of controversy about the interview between Emily Maitliss and Prince Andrew.

During my tenure, however. there was what I think has been the most damaging criticism of the BBC. Through all the various storms it has faced the BBC has, I believe, always tried hard to remain independent of the web of relationships between the great institutions of the establishment. The majority of the British people, myself included, recognise the need for the BBC, although it is a state institution, to be an independent broadcasting body. But the Iraq WMD affair and the subsequent Hutton inquiry caused a good deal of harm to the corporation. The Hutton findings caused the resignation of Director-General Greg Dyke and my colleague Gavyn Davies, a man unlucky to be Chairman at the wrong time. I will not go into the details of what happened because events have been recorded fully elsewhere. Suffice it to say that I thought we lost a good chairman and a good and forward-thinking Director-General over an overly critical inquiry report.

Having said that, I have read and believe the findings of a book written by former MP Norman Baker about the suspicious death of David Kelly. Kelly was the scientist who laid bare the fallacy of the weapons of mass destruction motivation for Tony Blair to send British troops to the Iraq War. It is my scientific background that leads me to be convinced that Kelly's exsanguination could not have been the result of the single small cut that was reported to have been made in the ulnar artery. An adult needs to lose about five pints of blood to die. This little artery, no thicker than a matchstick, would have drawn back from the wound, constricted and then clotted off.

To lose even a pint of blood in this way would have been unlikely. Kelly was an expert in lethal medicines and would have known all about this. There were also very disturbing inconsistencies in the evidence regarding how the corpse was positioned. The very fact that the file on this matter cannot be opened until 2103 makes me feel very uncomfortable.

Though I could not know it, the Board of Governors at the BBC was to be replaced by a body called The BBC Trust. This was the overseeing committee between 2007 and 2017. It was operationally independent of BBC management and external bodies, and its stated aim was to make decisions in the best interests of licence-fee payers. Then, on 12 May 2016, it was announced in the House of Commons that, under the next royal charter, the regulatory functions of the BBC Trust were to be transferred to Ofcom.

I have already hinted that my main concern as Welsh governor was those matters concerning Wales. Thus it made sense to join S4C when my time at the BBC came to an end. I had served a full term and though I was eligible to serve another term I detected that Rhodri Morgan was anxious to relieve me of my power. In some ways the first minister was a clever man but in other ways he was not so clever. He had a blind spot about some things. I was not too unhappy about giving up the role because I felt I was due some relaxation and I had other interests to pursue anyway, not least fishing. I had been so busy with work and public service that I had not had enough time to enjoy this favourite activity of mine.

At the time of my departure BBC Wales television was producing 15 hours a week of English language programmes within the schedules of BBC One and Two. We were also providing 10 hours a week of Welsh language programming for S4C, including some of its most popular programming like the BBC's oldest television soap, and flagship drama, *Pobol y Cwm*.

My main contribution to S4C was to deal with the rivalry between the two broadcasters. I told S4C that they were picking a fight with the BBC that they could not win, because of the corporation's vastly greater resources and that they should therefore desist from their incessant sniping. They resented, for instance, that it was the BBC who appointed the producers for *Pobol y Cwm*. They also had a hatred – I would put it that strongly – of dual language programming. I asked the S4C executives why they did not make programmes in both English and Welsh. They would be using the same actors, the same sets and the same props, so it would be very economical. The benefit in all likelihood would be to garner a much wider audience, both in Britain and abroad. I imagine most people would prefer to watch a drama that did not require dubbing. I also thought that attention should be paid to camera angles so that there would be minimal need for lip synching when a programme was dubbed. I like to think that my advocacy eventually bore fruit because dual language production now does take place.

I stayed at S4C for three years and I did not win every battle, but I think I may have contributed in some ways. The main problem concerned funding. Advertising revenue was paltry, because of small viewing numbers, sometimes as few as 70,000 people. Big companies were clearly not going to be attracted by such figures, though it was the case, and still is, that most adverts are in English. The Welsh government itself provided a fair amount of the revenue through its advertising for farm payments, vaccinations and so forth. The channel had a plan, Plan A, to increase revenue: lobby the government for more money. They did not have a Plan B.

My other media venture involved a private company called H&C TV. They got in touch with me before launching their television channel in 2018 because I had by then a reputation for knowing how to obtain funding from various sources. I say 'venture' but really it was only a short-term consultancy, for which I received no remuneration. I suppose I thought it might just be a good thing to do. They had decided to come to Wales to set up shop because they thought, as I had done with Penn Pharmaceuticals, it would be cheaper there than in some other parts of the country. They operated a minor channel on Sky at first, but now the channel is only available by subscription or through apps. The channel features equestrian matters and events. The thinking behind the formation of this company was that its programming would appeal to horse lovers and owners, the BMW brigade, so to speak. People who participate in dressage have to have a lot of money.

Speaking of a lot of money I should say something about my role as Chairman of the BBC Pension Trust. The pension fund was worth something like £15bn, which is more than some government departments get to spend. The fund's investments were run by one man, who was a retired accountant, who worked with the help of a single secretary. I found this terrifying, because if there had been a court case where I found myself interrogated about the wisdom of this arrangement, I would not have been able to say much. But I obeyed the age-old principle 'If it ain't bust, don't fix it.'

There might have been a huge risk in relying on this one elderly accountant, but I did my best to monitor how the money was being invested. I realise now that if he had come to an unfortunate end in some bizarre accident the stock exchange might have become affected. The advantage of having such limited oversight outweighed this unlikely risk, however, because it meant that I could easily access money to create offers that people could not refuse when it was felt that it was time for them to go. As chairman of the fund, I held sway, and no one was able to argue about the financial packages I put together to get rid of people who were long past their sell by date. Caesar had the power of the sword; I had the power of the biro.

I said earlier that I was first attracted to working with the BBC because of the talent that was there, but people do burn out, particularly good people. The brightest flames burn the shortest. Therefore, it was vital to have access to moneys that could be used to renew the pool of talent. I imagine that some people would recoil from the notion that the pension fund was being used for these purposes. They might recall the deviousness of Robert Maxwell, who looted the Mirror Group's pension fund of something like £450m. There is no necessity for such anxiety.

At the BBC we took care to use the fund as a type of reservoir, to be drawn from and to refill as and when it was wise to do so. If one is innocent of this common procedure, one might think that there was a risk of depletion of the fund, but it was not a case of selling stocks and repurchasing them, perhaps at a different rate. What happened was that there would be actuarial calculations of the amount of money necessary and this would be maintained by differing amounts of financial input each year. One year we might put £50m in; the next year perhaps nothing. We ensured that balance sheets were accurate throughout the process.

I have engaged in other public service too, but I shall return to those other roles later. Now I should revert to the field of pharmaceuticals and describe my endeavours in research and development as well as in sales and distribution.

Chapter 7 *Back to the Drawing Board*

I could have been a top notch spy. People confess the most amazing secrets to me, even when I'm not fishing for those nuggets
Jonathan Franklin

At the end of Chapter 5 I said that I would say more about the various companies I set up over the last twenty or so years. I had, to be clear, the capital I had raised by the sale of Penn Pharmaceuticals, but I also had capital from other sources. One of these was from the sale of a small chain of pharmacies that I had set up while I was working with Wellcome in the nineteen-seventies and nineteen-eighties. These pharmacies were trading as Lansdales and were located in the High Wycombe area. I seized the opportunity to acquire them when they came on the market because there were few restrictions in those days, and it was straightforward getting a contract to supply the NHS with medicines. Therefore, it was quite easy to expand quickly, and I also bought another pharmacy in the town. I could not really expand further afield, however, because I wanted to be reasonably hands-on and manage these businesses myself. I do not wish to say that I had any desire to get involved in the day-to-day business of dispensing drugs and medications, because I had had enough of that in Ruthin, but there were times when staff were unavailable because of sickness and so forth. Hence, I made myself available as the pharmacist of last resort and acted as locum when needed. The reason for my involving myself in the retail sector was that it was relatively easy to get credit from wholesalers and thus generate cashflow for my other trading enterprises.

It might appear as if I was stretching myself rather thin, setting up a number of businesses, but I was keen to develop technologies and improve pharmaceutical processes in a number of ways. My motives were not entirely pecuniary, I might add, though it would be immodest and not entirely true to claim that my motives were entirely altruistic. Actually, if one looks at certain websites, one will see a long list of my roles as board member and chairman of the board of a range of manufacturing and trading concerns. Such lists do not entirely accurately reflect my real operations, I have to say. During the first two decades of the new century, I was asked to join the board of a number of companies. I did join quite a few, though, looking back now, I am not sure how wise my decision was in some cases. The positions were invariably unremunerated, and though I felt I could bring a degree of expertise, both in specialist scientific terms and in terms of management and marketing experience, too often I had a sense that it was purely my name that was being sought.

E-Ster was a very different sort of company. It was a valuable enterprise that was trying to create a new technology for sterilising pharmaceutical products. Chemists up to this point were using gamma rays for the sterilisation process, but very often the dose deployed would destroy the product itself. As a result, people were using a process called aseptic manufacture, but this was far from perfect because there was always a risk of contamination. If you use ionising radiation generated by an electron beam, and apply it very carefully and precisely, you can control the process and achieve far better results.

At this stage in my career I had a lot of contacts across a broad spectrum of the pharmaceutical world, and significantly with UK regulators the Medicines Control Agency. Nowadays, plainly, as a result of widespread news reportage of vaccination protocols concerning Covid-19, we all know this agency as MHRA, I learned from my regulator associates that the Canadian government had lots of hydroelectric power and, since electricity cannot be stored, they had the idea to use their surplus power and convert it into an electron beam. They intended to build cyclotrons to conduct this work and they started to manufacture this particle accelerating equipment. As soon as I learned about what was happening, I realised what potential this could have in the UK, so I went over to Canada and bought one of these machines from the Canadian government. I knew the WDA were very anxious to develop this e-beam technology. Unfortunately, I was not able to get any grant funding, but I did get first option on a site in Mamhilad, near Pontypool. I planned to operate from there.

Things did not go to plan. The Canadians in The Atomic Energy Company of Canada had contrived a management buyout of this technology and I was told the machine I had ordered was the only one being built, and it was still in the construction stage. They then said that I could not take possession of it because they still had ownership. Clearly, I was never going to receive the machine, so I sold my rights to it to another company in Canada. I had paid cash, but all I had in return was a stake in the technology, in the form of share ownership. For a while I forgot about the matter, but, lo and behold, in the autumn of 2021 I received a letter from this second company in Canada, saying that they had sold their concern to an American consortium and that my shares were worth several million Canadian dollars. Not all of my ducks were always in a row; not all my ducks walked like a duck; this duck turned into a beautiful swan, however.

E-beam is now being used for sterilisation of pharmaceutical products, particularly those intended for injection purposes, because it is so much neater than using radioactive isotopes. The existing gamma ray technology involves having a conveyor belt of product circling a core of radioactive cobalt-60. This process continues until one can be assured of complete sterility. One problem with this approach is that the core is continuously decaying, and this creates too many variables. To guarantee absolute sterility you might have to give a dose perhaps ten times more than the desired dose. The e-beam, on the other hand, is a stream of electrons which can be applied with much greater precision.

Another company which looked like it would undertake important work was Alzeim, a local company based in Brecon. This company was working on a shoestring budget in the old hospital in

Talgarth but was in danger of going under. They knew from my work at Agropharm Ltd that I might be interested in trying to save the company, but in the event, I bought it from the Official Receiver after they went bankrupt. As the name suggests, the company was eager to research into the debilitating disease we know as Alzheimer's. And, though it might surprise the layman to hear it, the research involved the cultivation of daffodils. There is a lot to learn about daffodils for pharmaceutical purposes. There are several different species of daffodil, and they all produce interesting chemicals. Some species are especially significant because certain types will produce up to ten useful chemicals.

I set up Agroceuticals Ltd mainly with the intention of carrying out research into botanicals, so I was very interested in seeing if chemicals produced by daffodils could tackle, or at least mitigate, the effects of diseases like Alzheimer's. One of the chemicals isolated was galantamine, which hitherto was only produced synthetically. It is the only drug for Alzheimer's we have at the moment, though big pharma spends millions every year to try and discover a miraculous cure.

On studying the literature, we were able to note that the juice of certain daffodils also contained another chemical – narcyclazine – a powerful drug that stops glioma, a type of tumour which forms in the brain., though it can also affect the spinal cord. We are currently in the process of carrying out this exciting research at Cardiff University.

Despite the significance of our work, Agroceutical products is not a large-scale operation, only employing four people at a factory in Tredegar, incidentally on the same industrial estate as Penn Pharmaceuticals. Our purpose is not to create product for sale, but to conduct research. In this we are helped with a certain amount of grant funding. We also have an agreement with an American company that wants to include botanically sourced galantamine in one of their products. I am sorry to say it, but I fear there will never be a cure for Alzheimer's, but naturally people want to protect themselves from the worst effects of such terrible diseases, or even try to prevent contracting such conditions. Accordingly, there is a lot of money in preventative medicine. Notions of wellness are increasingly important, so pharmacists are recognising there is more money to be made in this field than in the field of treatment, in fact. It is hoped that products that contain galantamine will prevent the plaques which can build up and coat cells when neurons get entangled and fail to act as effective neurotransmitters. My main interest now is in this area.

I think I started out as a young man anxious to earn as much money as I could, but also to gain some authority and power, in order to improve whatever business I was involved in. I do not honestly think I ever really lost sight of my pharmaceutical ambitions, but these personal ambitions were always a very strong focus, particularly when I was spending most of my time trading, rather than conducting research. Now, in later life I am free to concentrate on the purer scientific aspects of work.

I mentioned that there are about ten chemicals in daffodils, and there is still a lot of work to be done to discover what these amazing little chemical factories may yield up in terms of medicines for human conditions. However, the work conducted at Agroceuticals does more than just that analysis.

There has been a certain amount of media coverage of the phenomenon commonly referred to as 'burping cows'. It is well known that cows emit a lot of methane when they pass wind. They also emit other pollutants when they burp. Their digestion produces, by way of a phenomenon known as enteric fermentation, ketones harmful to the atmosphere, in the same way that carbon dioxide is. Ketones are very simple chemicals; acetone would be a well-known example. In New Zealand, where the cow population is double the human population, there are plans to introduce a tax on cattle farmers because their stock is producing a greenhouse gas which is roughly twenty times more efficient at trapping the sun's heat than carbon dioxide

If you give certain elements of daffodil extract to cows, the production of ketones can be suppressed and there is less environmental pollution. A further advantage is that this ketone suppression aids milk production in dairy herds. Put simply, daffodils are helping us make cows more efficient! I should stress that this commercial advantage is just an extra benefit. The main point is that we should be paying increasing attention to the dangers of climate change. I do not believe that our politicians really understand the problem fully. I suppose it is inevitable when one has studied Humanities at university that one is five years behind the curve, so to speak.

As we all know, humanity's reliance on fossil fuels for over two hundred years has caused vast amounts of carbon dioxide to be released into the atmosphere. In my opinion we should be using offshore wind as an energy source. I cannot see any valid case that can be made against such wind farms. Tidal energy too is a fantastic resource for an island like Great Britain, with its enormous coastline. Not only is our coast longer than most countries – according to OS figures it is nearly twenty thousand miles long, if you include our islands – but it benefits from the surges of the Atlantic Ocean and the North Sea. Mediterranean countries may have impressive coastlines, but they patently work much better for tourism than energy production. I was part of the discussions about a tidal lagoon in Swansea while I was Pro-Chancellor of Swansea University. I am afraid to say that there was a lot of disinformation about the advantages and disadvantages of the scheme. I will say more about that in a later chapter.

As well as my business with Agroceuticals, I am still active as a director of a company called Morvus, which undertakes drug research. I am still chairman too of a company called Phytovation, which is based in Caernarfon. This company is involved with natural products such as senna. We buy in senna from two sources, one in India and one in Sudan. We de-seed the senna pods and mill them. Then, and this is the important part, we analyse and standardise the product so that it can be marketed in tablet form once it is bound with a binding agent like lactose. Of course, the senna plant has been used as a laxative for over thousands of years, but it has come to light that it is effective in treating the constipation which can occur as a result of taking opiates such as morphine and codeine. People taking such medication are suffering already, so it is of great benefit if they

92

can be spared the additional discomforts of constipation.

Yet another venture with which I was involved was with a company called Biofuels Wales. Aware of the perils of global warming and the follies of relying on fossil fuel, some bright people thought about possible botanical alternatives to gas and coal. We know that cane sugar has been used to make alcohol for a long time, and alcohol of course can be used as fuel, as well as a recreational lubricant. In fact, the petrol we buy at the pump today actually contains about 12% alcohol. Cane sugar is, of course, a type of grass, but unfortunately it does not grow in a UK climate. Now it would not make a great deal of sense to chop down trees in the Amazon rainforest to plant sugar cane and then ship it halfway across the world to produce alcohol in Europe. But if we could grow a similar grass, it would be different.

A lot of work was done in Wales to undertake selective breeding of grasses with a high sugar content, the thinking being that a high sugar grass could be used to make alcohol, which could then be used as a fuel. Academics at John Moores University in Liverpool tried to develop equipment which would operate like a microwave oven to break down the grasses and release the sugars to create alcohol. The grass used as hay fed to animals contains 8-9% sugar and the chemists did manage to raise this level to about 14%, but this was still well short of the 30% levels of sugar found in sugar cane. Economies of scale mean that it was eventually seen as not worthwhile pursuing these efforts at producing a viable source of sugar, and therefore alcohol.

Yet another idea I had, in what I thought of as my whiz kid days, was to tackle a problem which particularly afflicts the pharmaceutical industry, namely ensuring that things are perfectly clean. This normally involves putting things in an ultrasound bath, so I set up a company called Sonicclean in Rhyl in North Wales to try and design a better ultrasonic bath. Our attempts proved fruitless, however. Research is not always successful, but I think we should always try and think of better ways to do things to improve health, sanitation and medicine, so I try to weigh up my failures against my successes. Sometimes you fail, but it is important to fail better, as

Samuel Beckett puts it so tersely.

One issue that was exercising the minds of pharmaceutical researchers in the middle of the last century was the issue of creating a sedative which was non-barbiturate. Tens of thousands of people were dying each year because of barbiturate poisoning., largely because they were combining barbiturates and alcohol. In 1956 the German company Grunenthal developed a drug called thalidomide which did not contain barbiturates. It was understood of course that it had to be atoxic, but questions about rate of absorption were barely understood at that time. The solubility and the uptake by the body can vary considerably and this was the aspect of thalidomide that was not understood fully. The form of the drug that they developed at this time could not be absorbed. and was therefore passing straight through the gut.

To comprehend this fully one needs to understand the term polymorphism. This term refers to the way the molecules of a drug clump together to determine the rate of absorption, or indeed whether they can be absorbed at all. The German scientists were concentrating so much on the purity of the drugs that they failed to understand the importance of polymorphism.

The drug was sold over the counter and became a popular sedative. Soon it was marketed as a treatment for morning sickness. It had been tested on animals, and no animal died, but plainly not enough appropriate testing had been conducted on humans, certainly not pregnant women. By the mid-sixties it became obvious that there was an increased incidence of what is known as phocomelia, which is the condition of being born without limbs. It is a rare condition, thank goodness, only caused by one of two factors. One is a genetic disposition, but the other is as a result of a pregnant woman consuming a drug which is a teratogen, the name for any drug, metabolic agent, physical condition or infection which causes birth defects.

By the mid-sixties Thalidomide came to be recognised as a teratogen. It definitely caused babies to be born without limbs, or with truncated limbs. Sometimes fingers would be attached to shoulders, or toes to ankles. On occasion it is best not to know what

94

a Latin term means, but if I say that phocomelia derives from the Latin terms for 'seal' and 'limbs' one can see that the appearance of arms as flippers is the disturbingly accurate reason for the word.

I thought very hard about this highly contentious drug. Not everyone who was exposed to thalidomide was born deformed, but the true characteristic of a teratogen is that it will affect everybody exposed to its effects. There was a lot of variation in how pregnant women were affected by thalidomide because of what is known as bioavailability, the capacity of the drug to be absorbed by a patient. I tried to explain the phenomenon of how it was the case that there was not a 100% effect. There were several other bodies working in this area too.

One was Celgene, a new company working in The United States, who saw the value of thalidomide as a cancer treatment. It is currently licensed for certain treatments but there are dramatic warnings about its use for pregnant women, or any women who even stand a chance of becoming pregnant. For a while there was a crazy theory doing the rounds in textbooks that, because there are two ways in which molecules rotate when exposed to polarised light, it might be possible to isolate one of these types. The two types are called dextrorotatory and levorotatory, the Latin prefixes referring to right and left hand respectively. Some scientists thought that only the levo type caused the birth defects, so they tried to develop the dextro version, hoping to preclude any harmful effects. Several papers were written at the time expounding this theory. I got one of my young laboratory technicians to make me pure left and pure right versions. But, to my amazement, within hours they became left and right again through a process of dynamic equilibrium. Clearly the Americans' theory was not right.

I also developed a high specification type of charcoal. There were far too many cases of acute poisoning in the UK - typically young people overdosing on recreational substances - so it occurred to me that if we could get enough of an absorbent charcoal into the gut, we might be able to prevent a great deal of pain and damage. By using the intestinal wall as a semi-permeable membrane, the relatively higher concentration of the poison in the blood would be lowered in the gut because of the way that it would be locked up by the charcoal.

Charcoal is a very interesting material. Particle size and the source of the charcoal create a great variety in terms of the properties of the substance. Charcoal generated from bones, for example, is completely different from charcoal generated from twigs. To administer the charcoal, which of course is a solid, we would take a fifty gramme bottle filled with water and suspend in it particles of the appropriate charcoal. Patients would simply glug down a slightly gritty drink of water.

I do not keep up with the latest pharmaceutical research right across the board. There are subjects which interest me, and I try to keep up with those through the appropriate journals. One recent example I heard about is the self-cleaning material developed by Queen's University, Belfast. I have my doubts about miracle cure claims, however. How long does the cleaning last? How much does it cost to produce the material?

In 2011 I was appointed chairman of a public company called William Ransom and Son. Ransom had opened an essential oils extraction drug store as early as 1846 and the business quickly gained an international reputation for its commitment to quality. He believed, as do I, in helping his local economy by hiring local talent to work either in his lab or in the field (literally) collecting raw materials from the wild. His son Francis, a well-respected pharmacist himself, who had published several plant related articles, joined his father's business in 1913 and established Ransom's commitment to research and development.

After William and Francis passed away, Francis' son Richard, a botanist, took over the company. He had a keen interest in developing medicinal products from plants. This was an area I was eager to become more involved in. During Richard Ransom's tenure the company conducted research and also made its own finished products and sold them into the pharmaceutical and retail markets. A year after I joined, the company was acquired by OBG Pharmaceuticals; a privately owned company based in Liverpool. At this juncture it became known as Ransom Naturals Limited. Whilst firmly established in the pharmaceutical sector RNL also produces a wide range of extracts designed to deliver taste and functionality to food and drinks. Many of the beverages available in the retail sector contain a Ransom extract - elderflower is a great example.

William Ransom and Son had been a venerable company; one of the first companies registered on the UK stock exchange. I joined the company because I was very interested in creating drugs from plants, and I thought that some of the things I had learned by this stage in my career would be of value to the business. My time at Ransom Naturals was not profitable, however. The company was run by people who were too inexperienced in some important areas. Ransom bought plants and plant materials, but they knew very little about clinical trials for new drugs. The trouble was that they did not stick to their knitting. Foolishly they spent a small fortune trying to develop a product licence for an anti-arthritic drug called glucosamine. They were surprised when the work that they had done was discounted by the regulators. I came in hoping to be the guy with the white hat who would rescue the concern, but sadly Lazarus was dead and would not be aroused.

I intended to establish another company called Intellidose and I did register the name at Companies House. Unfortunately, it did not get much further than that. Here the idea I had was to design some sort of system for more accurate dosage of medical products. If you think about it, is it not strange that one person will take a 500mg tablet of paracetamol, yet another person with a completely different metabolism, body weight and size will also be prescribed the same dosage? It does not matter much in the case of paracetamol, evidently, but when it comes to antibiotics it really starts to matter. What was wanted, I considered, was a way to measure factors such as blood pressure, or indeed any measure of how a body was functioning, so that the speed of metabolism in an individual could be ascertained. This in turn could determine the timing or the amount of the next dose in a course of treatment.

I was ultimately unsuccessful in this enterprise, sad to say, because I could not access the sort of financial resources required. Also, in truth, it might have been the sort of work I would have had the energy to undertake when I was in my twenties, but by now I was in my early seventies. I am sure one day somebody will pursue this important line of research and make themselves a fortune. Not all my ducks were swans, though this one did try at least to be a cygnet.

The idea I had with Neuromind Biopharma Ltd, a company I set up in 2021, is that a person suffering from depression might take a single dose of psilosidin, a mind-altering drug like LSD, in order to wipe their mental whiteboard clean. This may sound like brainwashing, the controversial methodology of some totalitarian states in the nineteen sixties, and the stuff of science fiction fantasies, but it might be argued that the cleansing of bad elements in the brain, or psyche, might be preferable to the destructive powers of severe depression.

There is an increased level of self-reporting of mental disorders these days, but it does not mean that these disorders did not exist hitherto. When treatments were not available for people suffering from mental illness there was little point in talking about it. Once treatments become available, people are encouraged to come forward and seek them out. There is no quick pill that will resolve the issues associated with psychiatric conditions. It is very different from a sore throat. What is required is therapy with an experienced psychiatrist, if you need to unpick everything that has happened to an individual to cause him or her to be suffering. And there are two major problems: firstly, there are not enough practitioners and secondly, it would be horrendously expensive.

Some people are very sceptical about the vogue for therapy for the rich seen in so many Hollywood movies, but my own scepticism is more directed at those people who smoke huge doses of cannabis. Having noted the incidence of psychosis in people who indulge excessively, I thought it would be good to develop an antibody that would combine with cannabinoids to lock them away, figuratively speaking. This was a piece of research that I was aware was being undertaken by a small team during my time at Wellcome who were looking at monoclonal antibodies. These are antibodies which will only combine with one certain chemical. I was not directly involved with the actual research, but since I sat on a number of committees, including the medical and industrial research committees, I was able to see what was in the pipeline, what might come to fruition and what might not. It would have been catastrophically expensive to develop such an antibody though, and as I say, I am sceptical about the likely benefits for addictive personalities. Indeed, as one psychiatrist said to me, 'What's the point in changing the engine if the driver's going to wreck the replacement engine?'

I am also still active with a company initially called Zoobiotic, which now trades as Biomonde UK Ltd. Our chief interest here is in the cleansing powers of maggots. It was not me who discovered this, I hasten to add. It was known over the years that the maggots of the greenbottle would not eat live flesh, only dead flesh. The reason for this is that the maggots produce enzymes which break down dead tissue and turn it into a kind of soup. They then dine on the soup. In a way it is similar to the way that adult flies operate, expectorating over their food in order to make it easier to consume.

I could see that there would be a good market for a commodity which would be easy to produce but have considerable power to cleanse ulcerous wounds, so I decided to buy Zoobiotic from the NHS. Zoobiotic was a poorly run arm of the research side of the health service, manned by a small team of professionals who lacked the drive of true business people. They were surprised that they could not make any money out of their work, but probably not overly worried about it. The truth, however, is that though the NHS does not exist to make money it could not afford to haemorrhage it, as it was doing in this case. My purchase of this concern is, I believe, the only instance of denationalisation in Wales since the days of the labour government. It was sold because, like most other things in the NHS, it was being run inefficiently. People would come in and work when they felt like it, which is sometimes true of public servants who feel safe in their jobs, but much less prevalent in the private sector, where productivity is much more likely to be strictly monitored. This says more about my view of human nature than it does about any right-leaning political views I might be suspected of holding, I should add. As I have already said, it is difficult to be as idealistic as you were at twenty when you get older, but that does not mean everybody has to slide into wholly Conservative beliefs.

I bought the company as Zoobiotic, but I changed the name because I had the idea of having a whole series of animal products which could be used for the improvement of human health. Tape worms, for instance, I knew could be used as a highly effective way for obese people to lose masses of weight. This methodology is actually used in China today. Women who wish to remain petite take a capsule containing the head of a tapeworm. The consequence is that the food they then consume is snatched away by the parasite before it can be stored as fat. When these people, usually women as I say, have lost sufficient weight, or if they are experiencing discomfort, there are several drugs which can kill off the tapeworm and restore normality.

At Biomonde we have not pursued this particular avenue, but it was one of four or five notions I had as candidates for further research and development. As another idea, the use of hookworm was considered, but we are not currently pursuing any of these projects at Biomonde's base in Bridgend. There we currently produce little sachets of maggots, rather similar to teabags. Patients who, say, have an ulcer on their leg, tape the bag to the ulcerous spot and leave it for forty-eight hours. When they take it off again the wound is now clean. It is a brilliant idea, and it really does work.

I had decided that the best place to market this idea was in the USA. I borrowed money, incidentally, putting the company into substantial debt, to create a war chest of many millions of pounds in order to enter the US market. It was a big mistake, though perhaps if I had had hundreds of millions it might have been different. I was losing money and I was in danger of harming the good business we had in the UK and also in Germany. Realising I could forfeit a great deal, I cut my losses and got out of the States. It is a universal truth, as Jane Austen might say, that if you are building a business, you are taking trade away from somebody else. The facts of the matter were that the people we were taking business away from were strong, ruthless people, and I am sad to say, as corporate giants more of a match for the 'man in a shed in Tredegar'.

100

Chapter 8 *Back to School*

Look at where Jesus went to pick people. He didn't go to the colleges; he got guys off the fishing docks

Jeff Foxworthy

As I write this memoir the country is grieving over the death of the Queen. There is genuine feeling amongst a great swathe of the population that Elizabeth II was a great monarch. For my part, I am happy to think that the monarchy serves as the perfect foil against second rate politicians. The House of Lords is supposed to be a body that moderates the excesses of the House of Commons, but it is too political in its makeup. We know there are so-called crossbenchers, but every government tries to stack the odds in its own favour in its appointment of new peers. Queen Elizabeth II, I feel, served as a sort of block in the road, or warning sign at least, to stop politicians from doing whatever they like. Many people think that in The United Kingdom we are moving irrevocably closer to a more presidential system of government. Our history and our constitution, though it is not written, declare that our prime minister is *primus inter pares*, however, because the monarch has sovereign power. Thus, there are checks and balances, despite the weight and power of government,

I spent a lot of time with the new king, Charles III, when he was Prince of Wales and I have a high opinion of his abilities. Satirists over the years have depicted him as eccentric in some of his views but I know he is no fool. We met with some regularity when I was Chairman of the Training and Enterprise Council for Wales.

I decided we would support The Prince's Trust very strongly

and consequently he lobbied me for funding and for ideas about how to improve the facilities and opportunities offered by The Prince's Trust in Wales. The trust is a well-established organisation which provides education and training for young people who otherwise would not have training opportunities. One aspect of his interest certainly was his role as Prince of Wales, but he also recognised that there was a significant need for youth training in Wales because of the failures of the educational establishment.

It is a sad truth that too many Welsh schools were inferior to establishments east of Offa's Dyke. There was a palpable need for support because of the inadequacy of too many Welsh schools in terms of the provision of an aspirational impetus for disaffected youth. Schools and colleges were stressing the academic side of education at the expense of the encouragement of more practical skills. In Wales there was a need for vocational education and a range of apprenticeships, because manufacturing industries, in particular, relied on a cadre of well-trained labour. Clearly it was important that we retain these companies, and indeed persuade other such companies to set up shop where there was a constituency of well trained and motivated young people available as a workforce.

When I set up Penn Pharmaceuticals at my Tredegar base, I knew that I was saving up to a third of the costs of siting the facility in Southeast England. I decided, partly altruistically and partly pragmatically, that I would spend half of that saving on staff training schemes. The other half, of course, I was happy to trouser. This put me in a position where I could fund anybody who wanted time off to train in college. Anything remotely useful to the company was allowable. I had a staff of about a hundred who were all new to the pharmaceutical industry, many of them school leavers but many also previously unemployed people.

There was an existing training facility near Tredegar in Tafarnaubach trading estate which had been set up by a local councillor called Alan Davies. It did offer some training opportunities but there was poor discipline there, and as far as pharmaceuticals are concerned, discipline is key to success, both in research and production. There was also the much larger technical college in Ebbw Vale, only three miles away, but I did not think that the courses there were truly vocational in the sense that I realised was essential for my industry.

What I decided to do was appoint a full-time in-house training manager who would prepare training schedules for all staff. Everyone had a personalised training programme with short-term and mid-term goals clearly set out. To check what was working successfully and what was not working successfully there were regular six-monthly appraisal sessions. These monitored individuals' progress and training needs and allowed refinements where necessary. Of course, there is a saying that 'not everything that can be counted counts.' It is often attributed to Einstein, but I believe it was an aphorism coined by an American humourist by the name of William Bruce Cameron. He was primarily a children's writer, but he evidently knew something about formal rhetoric because he inverted the words, in a clever form of rhetorical device called antimetabole, to add 'not everything that counts can be counted.' I accept these wisdoms as a general principle, but I also know that counting things gives you certain guarantees.

In science, and certainly in the branch of science I know best, counting does count. The pharmaceutical industry has SOPs, or standard operating procedures. Every aspect of a job, down to the smallest minutiae, has to have an SOP. I would hesitate to think that some of my employees could ever write an essay about what they were doing in their pharmaceutical work, but they did know precisely what they were doing at every stage in their work. The specific training provided for them by our trainers at Penn was thus not academic, but it was highly effective. Trainers would provide employees with a standard operating procedure statement for the employees' individual work roles, but with certain key terms blanked out by Snopake. This typewriter correction fluid has been superseded by another fluid, so most people these days would think of us as having been Tipp-Exing the terms. The workers would have to fill in the blanks and date their response sheet. We could thus monitor the knowledge base of our employees.

I was pleased by the success of this regime but in point of fact I discovered that our rigorous training procedures was, if anything, too successful. Other employers noted that when they gave jobs to people who had left Penn, these workers had been properly trained and demonstrated admirable levels of discipline. Annoyingly, I found that it was public sector organisations who then began poaching our staff. I raised wages to try and combat such thievery, but that reduced the pot of money I had for training purposes, which was counterproductive.

I conducted the in-house training programme at Tredegar from the start of our production at the factory there. There were things happening in the outside world as well, however. A body known as The Manpower Services Commission had been set up by Prime Minister Edward Heath in the early nineteen seventies to try and do something about rising youth unemployment. The trouble, of course, with technical colleges was that they offered vocational courses without much recourse to data about the need for job-specific training in their catchment area. You might have a hairdressing course with a hundred or so students enrolled on it, but there might only be need for twenty hairdressers to join the profession at that stage. It was utter folly to think that eighty trained hairdressers were going to move to different towns to find jobs.

MSC lost its way rather and was eventually replaced by a series of private sector Training and Enterprise Councils, or TECs, established in the early nineteen nineties. People who ran companies in the private sector, who were patently more aware of the community's training needs, were given access to money to conduct training schemes. I was instrumental in setting up one of these, Gwent Training and Enterprise Council. There were only five such councils in Wales: one in North Wales, one in Mid Glamorgan, one in Powys and one in West Wales, plus the one in Gwent which I headed up. I was offered the opportunity to provide services for the whole of Gwent from our base in Newport.

What would happen was that companies would approach their TEC seeking a course of training applicable to their business. By and large the managing directors of the companies in Gwent chose us, rather than try to set up their own training schemes, because we had tutors who were experienced staff in the various trades and industries, rather than staff who had followed a purely academic educational avenue. I may seem overly robust in my opinions here, but I confess I found that people who had only had academic education were far less disciplined than those people who had learned on the job and/or through vocational training. There may seem to be a paradox, in that I was classically educated myself but spurned this form of education for my trainees and employees in favour of a much more vocational and less academic programme of study. The truth is that I demanded competence above all else. How can you teach competence if you are basically incompetent yourself? At least people should be able to record things, track things through, conduct proper assessments. All the Latin quotations and formal rhetorical devices in the world will not help in a situation that demands a practical solution. As evidence, although I do not wish to seem too controversial, I could point to the recent demise of a classically educated political leader. Sometimes one is judged on one's actions, rather than one's witty aphorisms or quotes from Pliny.

When Wales acquired some of its own political powers in 1998 the first thing the Welsh Assembly did was disband the TECs. It made no sense to me because these institutions were producing three times the outcome of previous vocational courses for half the price. We had the ability to compare. The Welsh government does not do comparisons; it hates them. We had a standard template for evaluating processes and outcomes. I am proud to say that Gwent TEC was regarded as the best TEC in Wales.

When it became obvious that Mid Glamorgan TEC was not succeeding, I was asked to take over. What we had learned in Gwent was transferred to Mid Glamorgan. This led to a merger and a new larger institution, Southeast Wales TEC, being formed. It involved moving everything to a site just north of Cardiff to handle trainees all the way from Bridgend to Newport. A lot of effort went into getting things right and establishing one of the biggest TECs in the whole of the UK. My reward for making a success of this venture was an OBE in the 1996 honours list. The award was for services to training and education. Obviously when one has a public face there is a degree of talent spotting, as it were, by politicians. I understand that it was somebody at the Assembly who put my name forward. The first thing I knew was when I received a letter asking if I was prepared to accept the honour. Naturally, I said yes.

Receiving my OBE was not the first occasion I had visited Buckingham Palace; I had attended a number of garden parties prior to that. I joked with friends that the royals were just checking that I did not eat my peas with my knife. Prince Charles, as he was then, presented me with my award with the generous words 'I have waited a long time to do this.' We knew each other reasonably well by that stage because of the financial help I had been able to provide The Prince's Trust from TEC funds. A typical case might be that we were alerted by a Women's Institute in Rhondda, say, that they knew of 16-year-old girls, now with their own children, who did not know what to do with potatoes other than fry them as chips. Cookery skills were essential. We found competent people to put courses together to teach these young people that there were healthier and more varied options. One day they might attempt potato dauphinoise, but at least they could for now cook boiled potatoes.

The secondary education system was failing young people, especially in the valleys towns and villages, because there were no expectations of success or even in some cases of employment. Truancy rates were high, and no one seemed to properly apprehend that it was skills and competence that were required, not just passing exams. I started thinking about the problem from the point of view of a potential employer, rather than from a pedagogical standpoint. How do you make a business grow? You need a toolmaker to fashion equipment to produce more, or to produce different items. The lack of mobility of people in small communities can be seen as an advantage that one can utilise. You have a trapped constituency of workers. Take an employer with a staff of just 10-20 providing services and products for other companies in South Wales. What is there to prevent you from expanding your sales area to Gloucestershire, or beyond?

A typical answer would be that the company finds it hard to get the people with the right skills. My response was to suggest a skills-based training programme. A business can thus grow organically. My successes were measured not only in the numbers of people being trained but the levels of competence achieved. The new National Vocational Qualification (NVQ) was the yardstick, rather than knowledge-based qualifications offered by schools and colleges.

The trainees, who previously had been disaffected school pupils bored by their curriculum and fully expecting to fail, liked this different form of education because it was relevant and offered the hope of not only a job but a better salaried job. I would counter an argument that we were narrowing down our trainees' opportunities for a broader and perhaps more profound educational experience by reference to the pragmatism that I have stated was always a strong principle of mine. The trainees wanted jobs; the employers wanted to make money. Wide vistas are fine things, but food on the table is a prerequisite.

At the other end of the educational spectrum, however, is the world of university education. I had not been part of the world of dreaming spires at Oxford and Cambridge myself and I did not dream of some sinecure as a professor of Business Studies, but I did want to get involved in some way with university management. I achieved my ambition in 2005.

Richard Davies was the vice-chancellor of Swansea University at this time, having replaced Sir Robin Williams, the very well-known astrophysicist, in 2003. Robin, who was christened Robert but always known as Robin, was one of my former Bala schoolmates and he had kept up with what I had been doing in Wales, as Chairman of the WDA, as BBC Governor and as Chair of the Welsh Training and Enterprise Council. He suggested I might be helpful to the university. I did not go through a formal selection procedure; I shared a few ideas with Richard Davies over a good glass of wine and was appointed Chair of Swansea University Council in 2005, a position I held till 2019.

The council is the university's governing body, which approves the mission and strategic vision; long-term academic and business plans; key performance indicators and overall standards of the university. The council assures that the university discharges its duties in accordance with the Welsh Quality Assessment Framework. It is composed of about twelve of the great and the good from both the public sector and the private sector. I have to say, it was difficult to get people in from the private sector because council meetings had been known to start at five o' clock in the afternoon and go on till nine at night. Realising this, I insisted that under my chairmanship no meeting would exceed an hour. At Penn Pharmaceuticals I actually physically removed the chairs from the meeting room after an hour had elapsed.

With meetings being held on a monthly basis and my rule that they would not go on past the hour mark, I was able to recruit people from the private sector as and when the old guard retired. I handpicked some people for their competence and experience, and above all their ability to sense if anything untoward was happening within the institution.

I talked about potatoes a couple of pages ago. I am reminded of a comment about potatoes made by a senior figure at Swansea University, The Dean of the School of Management. His remark, and various other opprobrious comments he made, caused me a certain amount of chagrin. Amongst his inflammatory utterances were some puerile comments made about trade unionists. I sometimes criticise colleagues myself, but I try at least to be elegant in my caustic comments.

The man who made the remarks was an academic called Nigel Piercy. He had come to Swansea in 2014 from Warwick University, ostensibly to improve the running of the business school. It is true that he had an impressive curriculum vitae and a wealth of highly regarded publications to his name. Vice-Chancellor Richard Davies had a particular skill in talent spotting, and he prised him away from Warwick with a very attractive financial package and also the offer of a position for his wife. The position as Dean of The Business School was, of course, advertised nationally but in truth he was the headhunted candidate and bound to get the job. I do not see much wrong with this practice because it is often the way to get the best

108

person. Unfortunately, Piercy would cause a good deal of trouble with his abrasive manner and outrageous opinions. I had no mandate to prevent his appointment, but I did tell Richard Davies that he should be very careful about the man. Richard preferred to keep him close, however.

It also came to light that abrasiveness and frank language was a family trait with the Piercys. Niall Piercy, Professor Piercy's son, was Pro-Dean of the School of Management. He had previously been employed as Chairman of Entrepreneurship in 2013. He too had considerable disregard for his colleagues, calling one former member of staff 'a worthless, lazy, amoral sack of human garbage'.

Both men were replaced. The elder Piercy's replacement was Marc Clement. Clement came across as a very intelligent and capable man, driven by his mission to improve the Business School and by his ambition to raise money for the university. Unfortunately, he proved to be unmanageable, however. When interrogated by the Vice-Chancellor about his ventures he was evasive, and I began to think of him as being more streetwise than business savvy. Suspicions grew that he also had ambitions to make a lot of money for himself and for his family and friends. This naturally could have been to the detriment of the university.

He set up a concern called Swansea Innovations, which was really only a means of obtaining money from the Welsh government, the UK government and the European Commission; money to fund various projects he had in mind. I was asked to be a director of this company and I agreed. As it transpired there were not very many board meetings, and the minutes of these meetings were not as full as one might expect. As a consequence, I had few dealings with the actual projects it generated and I realised my position as chairman was something of a token one, designed to add a certain veneer of respectability to what turned out to be a dubious set of enterprises. The most controversial of these was the plan to set up a Wellness Village in Carmarthenshire.

Details of his scheme are now a matter of public record because he was dismissed for gross misconduct for failing to declare an equity interest in the proposed £200m project. There was a protracted internal investigation and even a threat of police proceedings, though these were not instigated. Clement and a colleague involved in the scheme appealed against their sackings and they brought an unfair dismissal case to a tribunal in Cardiff. The tribunal found that the dismissals were fair and justified.

In my statement to the tribunal, I said that I knew Marc Clement relatively well and had known him since the days of the WDA. I stated that I had always found him very intelligent and plausible. I recall also stating that it was a biblical saying that no man can serve two masters and the saying was a pretty good one. The implication, of course, was that the appellants could not have served the university and Sterling Health, their commercial backer, at the same time. A Mr Laddie, the advocate for the university, claimed that it was apparent that I was completely believable when I said that I knew nothing about the jobs and potential shareholdings for a trust that Clement had said were his motivation. The trust never existed, and the project never got off the ground, needless to say.

The truth of the matter was that I was aware of the wellness village project and a proposed new university and private hospital joint venture for the university in Kuwait, but details were never disclosed to me, because they were very much early-stage proposals. I certainly knew nothing of the trust Clement and his allies were planning to set up for the enterprise in Carmarthenshire. Neither did I know at that time that the intended trust was likely to benefit individuals more than the university or the community.

Vice-Chancellor Richard Davies was very good at some aspects of his role, particularly the positives, but he was less equipped to deal with negative issues like the Clement affair. He received some notice for persuading Hillary Clinton to accept an honorary degree from the university, but he received a great deal of acclaim for his work at the helm of the project to create a new campus for the university in the regenerated area of Swansea on Fabian Way. This campus, which cost £450m, was a showpiece, brutalist architecture notwithstanding!

Richard Davies was a statistician by training. He was also dyslexic. Perhaps this gave him a creative edge, I do not know. I admired him anyway. I admired him but I fired him. By 2018 I had lost confidence in Richard's judgement. He had hired a chap from the civil service as assistant to the Vice-Chancellor, a man who had been in charge of Swansea's Vehicle Licensing Centre. He was a very competent man, but Richard began to think that he was coveting his job. I told him this was impossible because the man was a civil servant, not an academic. Richard's fears were not allayed, however and the university was no longer a happy ship.

He had always been very good at dealing with his political masters, successive government ministers, and he believed he was absolutely fireproof, especially because he had been so successful in building the new campus. The UK government had been calling for new build higher education facilities and he delivered. He had gained some EU funding but also a good deal of money from the private sector. The accommodation buildings were constructed entirely from private sector funding because the developers were happy to benefit from the rent students would be paying. Naturally in bright new accommodation rents were significantly higher than they had been in the old halls, and even in the city's commercial student lets.

The university had to dispose of its existing student accommodation in Hendrefoilan, a leafy suburb in Swansea West, and it did so very profitably, because the site was prime housing development land. We took care not to flood the market, which might have driven the price down, and the land was sold off in parcels. The point of selling off the Hendrefoilan accommodation was not to derive any pecuniary benefit for the university; the real advantages lay elsewhere.

Swansea had an enviable reputation for certain aspects of engineering courses and a few companies, Rolls Royce for example, were keen to be involved in course design and to recruit highly trained graduates. Swansea, of course, as a well-established redbrick university, had always offered degree courses in all the traditional subjects, but there was a sense that near-market courses in the latest technologies would be very attractive and profitable. And ultimately it suited the government's agenda to develop such technological expertise. Richard was happy to accept government capital funding, but my advice was not to accept the government's offer without a guarantee of further funds for maintenance of the buildings. This is sound commercial judgement, because the regular source of income, student tuition funding, barely covered staffing costs. As I told the Vice-Chancellor, we were in the education business, not the hotel business. Although there may be a case to be made that some students think in getting to university they have won a prize for a long stay at a large hotel.

I fear that the word 'competence' has somehow been side-lined in the world of higher education. Having focus, having purpose and knowing what you are doing are the key elements for success in life, and these are the learning outcomes I would desire from any level of education, but clearly very much so at university level. I do not think it matters very much what subjects you study, as long as the outcome is that you think more clearly, have a greater sense of direction and can apply yourself to whatever you choose to do with rigour and discipline. In the past I have used the analogy of the gunfighter. We are all gunfighters to some extent because we exist in a competitive world, but if you are not a very good gunfighter you get killed. There is, plainly, a place for philanthropy, the opposite of rivalry, in society too. In my experience, however, you need to make a significant amount of money through your competitive instincts to exercise your philanthropic wishes. The successful gunfighter can become the sheriff and the schoolmistress all in one; the unsuccessful one lies in the dirt outside the saloon.

I retired from my role as Chairman in 2019 because I was tired. I was also worried that my reputation could only be damaged by the difficulties caused by the Wellness Village affair and the sacking of Richard Davies.

Chapter 9 *Chairman of the Board*

I always felt that I would rather be out fishing or at home with my family than be at some cocktail party with a group of VIPs
Johnny Miller

In later life I have had a certain amount of time to pursue a number of interests in nature, music, education and even industrial buildings and little railways. I became involved with The National Trust, an institution close to my heart, because I understood that they were looking for someone to chair the Welsh committee.

The National Trust does a huge amount of good work for the environment, and all the people I encountered working for the trust were well meaning, it goes without saying. Unfortunately, as far as I was concerned, the organisation was not well run and lacked discipline. Administrators did realise at one stage that they were not doing much for industrial heritage. It was agreed that they should set up something called The Industrial Trust, to look after important buildings. I was asked to advise on such matters, so I played some small part in that work too, though not much was achieved, and it rather withered on the vine, in truth.

My involvement with The National Botanic Garden of Wales, which is something I still enjoy, dates from 2000, when I came across a wonderful character by the name of William Wilkins. William is an artist who lived near Llandeilo, but he had a fascination with the great houses built in Wales in the eighteenth and nineteenth centuries.

When the Napoleonic Wars put an end to the Grand Tour, the

rich decided to take their leisure in different parts of Britain, including Wales of course. They were drawn to the great estates naturally. Sadly, many of the houses fell into disrepair as neglect and death duties took their toll, but Wilkins set out to try and save as many of these as he could.

He did not worry too much about the new grand houses built by the coal barons because it was evident that their owners had made enough money for their upkeep. Rural establishments, on the other hand, became Wilkins' life's work. He discovered a house on the other side of Llandeilo, in a village called Llanarthne, and he made it the location of a Botanical Garden of Wales. The house is gone now, of course. Many of the old houses were burned down because their owners wanted the land but not the responsibility of maintaining the buildings. Pure vandalism, in my view.

Wilkins tried to bring these estates back to life, so he applied for government grants and established Wales's first Botanic Garden. There are several such gardens in England and Scotland, the most famous being Kew Gardens obviously, but others, including those attached to Oxford University and Cambridge University, long predated Kew. Such gardens are expensive to maintain and, though there are receipts from visitors paying at the turnstile, the Welsh Botanical Garden relies greatly on funding from non-governmental sources, such as The National Lottery. Also, private donations have come to its aid.

There was a scheme whereby the government funded 95% of the costs of a public utility if the charitable sector could find 5% of the funding. Finding even that 5% proved very difficult, however. There are certain restrictions about where the 5% comes from, for instance it has to come from taxed income. Ann and I decided to donate a significant sum to help set up the project, because we are very enthusiastic about improving public knowledge of nature and the environment. This met the criteria for the utility to draw down the remaining 95%. I might have had cause to regret my benevolence, I must say, when I discovered that the management did not even keep a record of this gift! Despite this, I am still happy to have been a major sponsor of this worthwhile cause.

114

I have said something about my fishing interests, and I will elaborate on this activity further in due course. For now, since I am describing my work on committees and boards, I should mention that I tried to support the Carmarthenshire Rivers Trust. The trust was getting money from Welsh Water, as a result of the disruption to fishing caused by the construction of the Llyn Brianne dam in the early nineteen seventies. The Trust spent this annual amount ostensibly making improvements in the fencing next to the River Tywi and its tributary River Cothi. I have never been entirely clear what real benefits arose from this expenditure, I have to admit. Anarchy rules in Wales and I lost interest in the Trust eventually.

Another disaster was the Cardiff International Festival of Musical Theatre. I had been heavily involved in the Cardiff Singer of the World competition because of my BBC connections and the continuing significance of this event is something that pleases me greatly. Cardiff Council had the idea to establish a similar event for show songs, a genre for which I have always had a great fondness. We found a sponsor, the Thomas family, who put up a couple of hundred thousand pounds, and we managed to raise some other moneys from various other trusts. I did not contribute on this occasion, but the Welsh government declared that they would be happy to be involved.

The event took place three times over a period of six years but there was difficulty in getting backing, despite the calibre of the competitors. It was televised on one occasion but viewing figures were poor and the BBC decided to discontinue televising it. This was curtains for this little brainchild, I'm sorry to say.

The Learned Society of Wales was something I set up, strangely enough with Marc Clement riding shotgun. Clement saw the value of this body in terms of his own efforts regarding fundraising. My reasoning was that Scotland had its own Learned Society and Wales would benefit from such a group of professionals and academics. After devolved powers came to Wales, however, the Assembly, in its wisdom, was of a mind that AMs did not need advice from such an extraneous body. Our aim, nevertheless, was to bring in experts in particular fields, usually retired academics in science, arts and humanities subjects, to contribute as consultants over government projects. Sometimes too it was useful to call upon the expertise of professionals in the legal sphere. The society is still in existence and has a CEO who decides what issues require attention, with members meeting once a quarter to address these issues.

There was a lot of expertise available from members of The Learned Society when it came to projects such as the Swansea Lagoon. The lagoon was a private sector proposal from a company which, amongst other enterprises, ran a quarry on the South coast. They had the bright idea that if they could ship their stone up the Severn Estuary, they could build a barrage using their own materials. The tidal reach in Swansea of nearly thirty-two feet is second only to The Bay of Fundy in Nova Scotia, so there is huge potential for tidal energy production. But, as always, there is a downside.

I had been happy to see the idea of the Severn Estuary barrage being abandoned, because in my opinion it was a stupid idea. The harm it would have caused to the environment, and especially to migratory fish, was incalculable. When I say migratory fish people usually think just of salmon but there are other species which would have been affected, such as scad. This may be strictly fisherman's knowledge, but scad are a type of mackerel that provide a major food source for some cultures abroad, though not so much for the British market. They are thus a valuable commodity in themselves, but they are also an important food source for seabirds and some larger fish.

As far as the Swansea lagoon was concerned it was a slightly different matter. Environmentalists were still keen to stress the effects on migratory fish, but I felt the numbers involved in the bay were far less significant than in the Bristol Channel. There was clearly an emotional impact on public opinion, however, when environmentalists pointed out how fish would be mutilated by the turbines as they tried to pass through the barrage walls.

The lagoon was never built, largely because the proposers of the scheme wanted too much for themselves. They pitched their scheme to the Welsh government, who agreed that further research could be undertaken, but the funds the company said they required proved far in excess of what was available.

There were no particular objections to the scheme on aesthetic grounds and I have to declare that I was a supporter because of the job opportunities the project would have created, plus the enormous benefits of a natural energy source which would have powered a huge stretch of the South Wales coastal belt. The amount of electricity generated was not going to be enough to meet the costs of building the lagoon, was the eventual decision. It seems a missed opportunity to me now that the arrogance of certain Welsh politicians held sway when recent price hikes in energy and an increasing concern about the damage that a reliance on fossil fuels causes in terms of climate change have caused so much consternation in the British public.

The present-day political leaders in Wales are, it appears to me, not a huge improvement either. I will refrain from controversy though and say no more on that subject.

Another little venture I participated in elevated me to the lofty position of President of The North Wales Coastal Railway, a narrow-gauge little train company. A scientist friend of mine, Professor Tony Atkinson, had a serious interest in railways. He bought the Fairbourne railway, which runs from the village of Fairbourne in North Wales to Barmouth on the West coast. He used his own funds, though he was helped to some extent by his colleague Dr Roger Melton. He had to continually subsidise the concern because it was never a profitable one, so he obviously wanted some financial support to maintain the railway. He asked for my help, knowing that I had experience in garnering funds from a number of sources. In this particular case he wanted me to approach the Welsh government.

I have to say my experience with the North Wales Coastal Railway was not a particularly edifying one. The railway itself is a nice little affair, but the people involved, retired engineers and so forth, were what our American cousins tend to call 'hayseeds'. Again, enthusiasm is no great substitute for sound financial sense and rigour.

I remarked earlier that my love of show tunes led me to get involved with a musical theatre competition. I also said that I loved jazz when I was a teenager. This love led me to get involved with a

117

remarkable venture, the Brecon International Jazz Festival. It was something of a phenomenon in the world of music for a small town like Brecon to host a whole weekend of performances from musicians with a global reach. As it happened, George Melly, who was a TV personality as well as jazz singer, lived close by and became a supporter. Huge names in jazz music happily came to play, in the same manner that international rock stars go to Glastonbury to perform these days. Glastonbury is essentially a field in Somerset, so you might think that Brecon would be a better venue for a range of musicians. In my opinion, however, it was a mistake to locate the event in the centre of Brecon. There is not a satisfactory focal point in the town, so what happened was that various pubs set up their own jazz events and everything became disjointed, not to say discordant. Frankly, I thought it came to resemble a car crash, and I had had enough of those in my early twenties. It was difficult to put a cohesive programme together and I had concerns about how income control operated too. A bigger arena would have helped.

I suggested that the festival should be moved to Builth Wells, where there is a large showground used for all sorts of events, such as dog shows, country fairs, agricultural shows and a host of other activities. Builth is only fifteen miles from Brecon, so it would have been feasible to still call the weekend the Brecon International Festival. My suggestion sadly fell on deaf ears. I did stay involved with the festival for four or five years, as a member of the organising committee, but I have lost touch somewhat these days.

Though I do not go to the festival any longer, I love jazz. I wish I could play a musical instrument, but I cannot, never really having had time to devote to learning to play more than a few basic guitar chords. When I listen to Dave Brubeck, always a favourite artist of mine, I am stunned by the invention and the virtuosity of his music. His style is unique and very different from the 'trad jazz' musicians of the early sixties who I mentioned previously, but I feel eclectic taste is no bad thing. These days I will also happily listen to more modern forms of jazz when I hear them on the radio. Dizzy Gillespie's trumpet playing and Thelonius Monk's piano playing thrill me and pacify me equally, if that makes sense.

While still operating in the TEC sphere I was a director of a body called Investors in People. An award from this body functioned as a major incentive for TECs to persuade industries to use their facilities to train personnel. Our trainers would advise the managers of firms on the sort of training that would be suitable for their staff and what would qualify their businesses to wear the IIP badge. You see this award displayed proudly outside all sorts of institutions and businesses. University of Glasgow research in 2019 actually found that 78% of employers found that undertaking training which led to the award had a 'positive' or 'very positive' impact on their organisation.

If anyone outside Wales was interested enough to look at the list of committees and boards I have sat on or chaired over the years they would see that I also sat on two Welsh committees, Cymdeithas Genweinwyr Gwalia Cyf and Elusen Gwyl Y Faenol. A mouthful for a non-Welsh speaker, but easily translated.

The first of these committees relates to fly fishing. John Elfed Jones, the former chair of Welsh Water I have already mentioned as a colleague of mine, set up Cymdeithas Genweinwyr Gwalia Cyf in Bridgend as a private company and invited me to join as a director. The business involves looking after the interests of freshwater water fly fishing devotees.

The second committee, Elusen Gwyl Y Faenol, or Faenol Festival Trust, concerned a venture set up by the internationally renowned bass baritone Bryn Terfel. Bryn is a brilliant singer but perhaps not truly a businessman, at least in the sense that I have of that term. There is a big estate just outside Bangor called Y Faenol, and Terfel and his management team thought it would be a good idea to erect a big marquee there and hold an annual opera music festival. Because of his fame he was able to persuade an impressive range of huge international stars to appear, including the world-renowned Italian tenor, Andrea Bocelli. Terfel's management team were very anxious to get their hands on WDA money to help finance the project, but I found it exceedingly difficult to access their accounts. The trust is no longer in existence, but Bryn Terfel also created a scholarship scheme to promote young opera singers in Wales, and latterly also internationally. This is a thriving scheme, though the award is not huge in money terms, and is now part-funded by the Welsh government.

Chapter 10 *The Good, the Bad and the Ugly*

Many men go fishing all their lives without knowing that it is not fish they are after

Henry David Thoreau

There is a song called 'Common People' by nineties band Pulp which has the refrain:

I wanna live like common people
I wanna do whatever common people do

I must say that was never my aim in life. No one knows exactly what they are going to do, of course, as they fret about growing up, then fret about how hard it is to establish yourself and your station in life, then all too often look back and fret about what it was that you actually did or did not do. For most people it is not a remarkable list of personal achievements. When you ask somebody what the highlights of their life are, they will tell you about the birth of their first child perhaps, or their amazing wedding day. They might even speak about their job or their wealth. They may also boast about famous people they have met.

I have no boastful intentions here. I have indeed met a lot of famous people, but such encounters have not always been wonderfully edifying. One character in particular I do need to mention, and I do with considerable distaste. I am talking about the odious Jimmy Savile.

I met him on more than one occasion. I did not realise it, but he was a member of my club, The Athenæum. Amazingly, he was put up for membership by the Archbishop of Westminster. I must say I was surprised, because the club was founded nearly two hundred years ago as a meeting place for artists, writers, and scientists, with a few bishops, judges and senior politicians, not necessarily of any one party, thrown in. The idea of the club was to nurture civilised conversation and companionship; provide superb library facilities, and offer members the opportunity to attend high quality cultural and social events. I could not quite see how Savile would gain anything from any of these benefits. Nor could I see him as contributing very much to the intellectual and cultural discourse of the members. Anyone who drives around in a gold Rolls Royce and wears a gold medallion the size of a medium dinner plate, I felt, would be unlikely to add to the tone of the club.

In what seems to be a peculiar blindness to the moral vacuum that was Jimmy Savile, both Margaret Thatcher and Prince Charles were most fulsome in their praise for his work for charity and for his self-promotion as the ordinary man made good. Indeed, the whole country appeared to be in his thrall. The recent BBC documentary by David Dimbleby I referred to in Chapter 6 highlighted the paradox that he was universally popular but also widely suspected of having a very dark side to his character.

Some of the producers at the BBC wanted to use Jimmy Savile as a presenter of *Children in Need*, presumably to boost viewer ratings, and I was asked, as Chairman, if I thought it was a good idea. I felt very protective of the charity, and I was very unsure about Savile's probity. I talked to some of the team operating the *Children in Need* foundation and they told me to do my own research. I took this to be a veiled warning.

One of the occasions where we crossed paths, and it was no more than that, was at a cocktail party at the BBC whilst he was still flavour of the month. It was one of the many many cocktail parties producers held. To be candid, it could be said that the BBC at that time floated on wine.

I was chairman of *Children in Need* from 1999 to 2002 and, with the scepticism of the team reinforcing my own suspicions, I refused to let Savile anywhere near the appeal. I actually said to one interviewer 'I think we all recognised he was a pretty creepy sort of character.' We most definitely stepped up our child protection policies and this would have put him at risk if he tried anything.

I found Savile's behaviour very strange. I could not tell if he was a paedophile, but I did not have to. I told those people who questioned my decision, 'If you're going to go on the attack and make claims against him then you'd need evidence – hard evidence that simply wasn't there. But if you're protecting yourself, you can do that without evidence.' I am fairly certain that he was not the only paedophile attracted to the telethon either. Unsavoury characters were drawn to such events like flies to a honey pot. Not just in the fundraising aspects but also in the distribution of funds.

Much later I felt bound to criticise the then Director-General, George Entwistle, for failing to ascertain details of a Newsnight investigation into allegations of child abuse by Savile. He gave the go-ahead to broadcast tribute programmes to the presenter after he had died in 2011. Rumours were circulating everywhere about the crimes of the despicable DJ and TV personality, but Entwhistle did not ask the question 'Why?' when Savile was pushing for the opportunity to be with children. I found that extraordinary, and I told the press so. I added that I would have stepped down from my *Children in Need* role if Savile had been allowed to become involved with the charity.

By contrast, I have met some very decent people and some fascinating personalities. In part this was as a result of working at the BBC. Gavyn Davies was one. He had been a leading figure in finance as a partner in Goldman Sachs, one of the big five investment companies in the USA. When we met, he had become the Chairman of the Board of Governors at the BBC. We got on particularly well. I count him as a fellow Welshman because his parents were born in Aberystwyth, although he was not Welsh speaking. He was married to Gordon Brown's Personal Assistant and therefore he had strong connections to the Labour Party. Labour politicians wanted to keep tabs on the BBC, especially during the difficult days of the Hutton Inquiry.

I got on less well with my successor, Merfyn Jones, who had been the Vice-Chancellor of Bangor University. He was more of a party apparatchik. He used to go hill walking with Dai Havard, the

MP for Merthyr. He also became chair of Betsi Cadwalladr Health Board, which had to be placed in special measures in 2015, when an enquiry found that the treatment of mental health patients was highly unsatisfactory, not to say dangerously incompetent. A report disclosed that vulnerable people were placed in close contact with drug abusers at Hergest mental health unit in Bangor, causing great distress and even a number of suicides.

Some of my other acquaintances at the BBC were very impressive, however. Richard Eyre, for instance, was a good man. He was the drama specialist for the BBC board of governors. He spoke well and intelligently on a number of subjects and, something of a rarity, I would say he was apolitical.

Equally impressive, if not more so, was the TV and radio personality Terry Wogan, whom I got to know quite well. He was a very intelligent man, with great charm and no perceptible ego, something not often found amongst the very famous.

While I was Chairman of the board of *Children in Need,* I was suspicious of a number of parties who were anxious to get involved, or keen at least to get their hands on cash raised through the annual telethons. Unfortunately, not everyone who declares that they are driven to help children with learning difficulties, for instance, has the purest of motives. Of course, it was difficult to prove what these people's intentions were before they had actually performed any acts against these children. I encouraged the people working on *Children in Need* to make every effort to find out if these dubious characters, who were claiming that they wanted to help with the fundraising, were wearing black hats or white hats. I am always amazed that there are so many evil people in this world. I should qualify that: I am amazed that there are so many people in this world who are sexually attracted to children. It is not for me to offer moral or psychological judgements here. The men who preyed on children sometimes presented themselves as individuals, but frequently they would be people who had set up what were supposed to be charities whose purpose was to help deprived or vulnerable children. Such were the levels of hypocrisy.

A problem arose because, though *Children in Need* had been

entirely a BBC project from the start, some producers wanted to do something different. They posed the question why not do something like *Comic Relief*, that is, make it a national charity event, with the BBC merely acting as a means to televise proceedings, rather than organising everything. In this way I guess they hoped to deflect potential criticism. I rejected this suggestion because I thought it was important to maintain control over things, and it was by no means certain that the BBC would avoid the flak if there was controversy. Such controversy of course would be likely to centre on the disposal of moneys raised. It is comparatively easy to raise money; it is more difficult to arrange for its distribution if dodgy charities are circling you. The dispute was quite a heated one. But importantly, Terry Wogan backed my judgement. And I do not think that it was a matter of pride regarding his prominence as the presenter which motivated him, for he was essentially a humble man. In fact, I know his heart was really in the efforts we were making to help children. I was surprised and pleased how insistent he was in supporting my views. Nevertheless, there was some serious conflict between the board and some of the senior executives and producers at the BBC. I may be overcritical here, but I got the impression that for some people the reflected glory of consorting with major celebrities was more important than the actual charity work.

I dined with Terry Wogan at his club, The Groucho Club. He would sometimes stay there overnight of course. I am not a member there, but I have often stayed overnight at my own club, The Athenæum. If you are fortunate enough to be proposed as a member of one of the better institutions it is very satisfying that you are guaranteed a good room and excellent dining facilities, rather than having to chance your luck at a central London hotel, indeed if you can find one with vacancies. For those readers who are unfamiliar with the etiquette of London clubs, I should say that the impression that might be gained from television dramas and depictions in films about the way that they operate could be a false one. The staff at my own club certainly, but I felt it was true at The Groucho as well, were by no means over-deferential or obsequious. On the contrary, they could behave with schoolmasterly strictness about attire and so forth.

I have to say that my relationship with Terry Wogan was not a close friendship, though I did have the privilege to attend the Westminster Abbey funeral of this much revered man. Rather, I enjoyed the meeting of minds about how we should go about things at the corporation. The BBC is a strange institution and can at times be quite oppressive. He felt he could offer me his support, and the support of his circle of friends and allies, over decisions such as the future of *Children in Need*.

I met lots of famous men and women during my time at the BBC. Having said this, I confess I did not seek out the company of some of the shallower figures of the pop world or the sporting world. Maybe I am too aloof in these matters, but I am chary of spending too much time with people who are not likely to contribute much to human knowledge. I am not dismissing all singers and footballers here, I hasten to add. I met Kathryn Jenkins and found her to be a lovely bubbly personality. Actually, I made a television appearance with her on a chat show once on S4C and found her to be both intelligent and cogent.

Many celebrities are nothing like as arrogant and conceited as they might appear on screen. Jeremy Paxman, for instance, I think prided himself on his disdainful demeanour as an interviewer and also as a host on *University Challenge*, but on the occasions I spent time with him, on train journeys from Cardiff to London, for example, he came across as rather reticent, and even nervous. He would not say anything controversial, and he seemed as if he was prepared to agree with anything I had to say. This might have been because my position as a governor of his employing body made him think that what he said might not earn him any merit points, but it might earn him a demerit. The simple truth is that producers would tell presenters what they could do and what they could not do by saying something like, 'The governors will never allow that.' It was the 'It isn't me, it's my brother' approach to control. Thus I was accorded a lot more respect than I probably deserved. All too often presenters who came across as supremely confident characters in front of the camera harboured serious concerns about how their career might proceed, or stumble, if they offended people in my position. There was no truth behind their suspicion that I held their fate in my hands, of course. It was the Director-General they really had to be afraid of.

David Attenborough was a wonderful man, but again I found him very deferential. These days he is obviously best known for his nature documentary programmes, the marvellous *Life* series, but he had been Controller of BBC Two and Director of Programming for BBC Television during the nineteen sixties and seventies, so he was a man of considerable substance. I met him fairly frequently at BBC parties and found him most companionable.

Gary Lineker was perhaps not quite as deferential. Possibly it is true that athletes of the highest calibre are relatively less impressed by people who are not quite in the same peak physical condition. Anyway, I found Lineker intelligent, well informed, articulate and easy to get along with. Not qualities I would always associate with footballers, whose IQ is sometimes equivalent to the number of tattoos they are sporting. Being a sports broadcaster, his main concern was the value of football coverage to BBC1. Sadly, the hegemony the corporation had enjoyed for decades was under serious threat, not just from other terrestrial channels but from the might and money of one man, Rupert Murdoch. He had huge resources and a clear plan of action in his attempts to dominate the media. I have met several people who have stated that they would never have wanted to subscribe to Sky TV, but felt they had to, if they were ever going to see coverage of the sport they loved so much. Murdoch even purloined cricket from the BBC too, of course.

Some of the finest people I have met have been those involved in charity work. I should mention here that I have fairly recently become involved with Maggie's, the cancer charity. Maggie Keswick Jencks was a woman who contracted cancer and, when told that her condition had returned, found herself left in a windowless corridor to process her consultant's news. She discussed with her husband the need for somewhere 'better' for people with cancer to go. She then set up a chain of spaces where people with the disease could discuss their issues with highly trained oncology nurses and other fellow sufferers. Maggie was an architect and wanted the meeting places to be a little more inspiring than the normal drab venues you might expect in public sector buildings. One excellent aspect of her design was that centres should appear warm and welcoming and have a walk-in policy, rather than an appointment-based system. She had built a centre in Swansea at Singleton Hospital, but it was decided that it would be a good idea to establish another space in Cardiff, at Velindre Cancer Centre.

I became Chairman of Maggie's Wales and I set myself the task of raising three and a half million pounds for the initial building cost. This might seem a lot of money, but every Maggie's centre is unique in its architectural design and one of the main criteria for the architects appointed was to avoid an institutional look and feel. When you are at a low ebb a desk and three hardback chairs is not necessarily a sympathetic environment. Understanding this, Maggie's in Cardiff had what we call in Wales a 'cwtch', a small and more private area where one could take one's ease quietly and comfortably.

I went to Velindre with Ann, and we agreed that it was a desolate sort of place, scarcely different from an industrial portacabin, with Blu-Tac holding notices to the wall. It hardly allowed people to think that they were being held in high regard. Hence, I was attracted to the cause, not least because Ann had had cancer herself. I managed to raise the money, a good deal of it through the aegis of the Welsh Assembly. There were also a few private sector donors. These were individuals rather than companies, because there are many people who understand the privations of the awful disease and its sometimes brutal therapies.

Some of the most invidious people I have met have been politicians, as may be becoming evident in this narrative. Perhaps I should not name names, but I will admit that I did not have much time for Chris Patten or John Redwood. Anyone who is Minister of State for Wales who tries unsuccessfully to mime the words of the Welsh national anthem, and is televised doing so, is not someone I am likely to admire greatly. I knew Redwood during my time at the Training and Enterprise Councils. He called me in for a meeting once and I found I was seated intimidatingly on one side of a huge table, with Redwood opposite me and his several henchmen sitting like guard dogs at either end of this table. On two separate occasions I was in the middle of speaking when he cut across me. I said to him, 'I think I am the only one here who is not being paid to be here. If you are not prepared to listen, I may as well leave.' I got up and walked out, followed by his guard dogs, who tried to persuade me to return. They were unsuccessful. Redwood had got a few facts which he was chewing on, but apparently with some distaste, and I was reminded of a rather nervy ruminant in a field chewing on damp hay.

I remember him visiting the Gwent TEC. He wanted the meeting at 5.00pm one Friday. When he arrived, I greeted him cordially enough and told him I was pleased that he had found time to join us on his way home to his constituency, where he would doubtless be able to enjoy a gin and tonic after work. He spat out his rejoinder: 'I never want to hear the words "gin and tonic" and "constituency" in the same sentence!' To this day I am unclear about the nature of my offence.

I did, however, enjoy the company of Ted Rowlands, the Merthyr MP who was active in the Foreign Office for a number of years. Ted was a fellow Welshman who did a lot for his constituency and indeed for Welsh affairs. He and Peter Hain, of whom more in a moment, were tremendous advocates for the anti-apartheid movement which ultimately led to desegregation in South Africa.

I had some dealings with Ed Balls, who was Secretary of State for Children, Schools and Families in the Labour government and later Shadow Chancellor of the Exchequer. Such is the power of television, people nowadays are more likely to remember him for his exploits on *Strictly Come Dancing* more than his political achievements, I fear. I had given him a sheet of A4 with various of my achievements listed on it, with the hope that he would bear them in mind when it came to considering who might appear on the next honours list. In truth you could say I nobbled him, and the aforementioned Peter Hain, who had become Secretary of State for Wales, in my attempts to gain a little recognition for my efforts. I must say, Peter Hain was a much more effective Welsh secretary than his predecessors John Redwood and William Hague, both of whom, I suspect, had other fish to fry than the wellbeing of people in Wales.

The best of the Welsh politicians with whom I had dealings was Ron Davies. He was a man who did not take prisoners. He actually kept a little notebook, and it was wise to avoid having your name added to the personal hate list I think he must have kept in there. He had a fine mind, however. His political career unfortunately came to grief over 'a moment of madness', as he termed it. The incident took place on Clapham Common, notorious for gay encounters, when he was mugged at knifepoint by a man he had approached. It is often the case that what undoes a public figure is not a transgression but the excuse or the untruth which attempts to explain it or dismiss it. So it was with Ron Davies, who subsequently emerged from a wooded area by the M4, it is presumed after an intimate encounter, with the explanation that he 'was looking for badgers.' His account was derided by the public, naturally. I think it was a shame that he fell from grace because he was a fine politician and advocate for Wales.

Neil Kinnock was also a highly regarded figure in some quarters, but I tended to think that he substituted volubility for true insight. He was a good orator, but rhetoric needs substance. He had been in university at the same time as me, as had his future wife Glenys, but I did not know them well then. It was, however, a point of connection when we met in later life. After he left parliament, he did get in touch with me occasionally, usually to try and persuade me to donate to the brass band he was connected to in Ebbw Vale. Despite my love of a great range of different musical genres I declined to offer my support. Loud wind instruments can jar at times.

I think politicians are prone to a belief that there is a huge money mountain and all they have to do is mine it and ask for more, but life is not like that. They do not realise how hard it is to make the money in the first place. I think it is faintly amusing that Theresa May insisted that there was no magic money tree, but subsequent Conservative Prime Ministers apparently magically discovered one. They are not alone in their conviction that such sources for expenditure exist, I sometimes reflect, especially when my wife tries to persuade me that we need some new extravagant consumer items!

I have only spoken about Labour and Conservative politicians so far. For the sake of fairness, I should mention that I had cause to meet a leading figure in the Liberal Democrat party too, a man by the name of Lembit Opik.

I need to provide a little background here. Whilst in university I went to folk music clubs and there were quite a few aficionados of this type of music. Some very wealthy people had fled their homeland, Estonia, in the 1940s, when Russia occupied their country, and when they arrived in Wales they established an Estonian club in Cardiff. I got to know some of these people and always had a fondness for Estonia as a country. So much so that I was eventually asked to become Consul in Wales to The Republic of Estonia.

It may be surprising to some but there has always been a strong trading connection between the two countries. Estonian timber was a valuable commodity because it had a history of being used for pit props in Welsh mines. Estonia in turn was keen to trade their lumber for engine parts and other industrial produce.

Lembit Opik is of Estonian extraction, and he was quite well known in Estonia. Indeed, at one point he considered standing for president of the country. He is, no doubt as many people know, a very colourful character. He also attempted to stand as President of the Liberal Democratic Party and later for the position of Mayor of London. He did eventually manage to become a chairman of a political party - the Party of the Space Kingdom of Asgardia. This so-called 'micronation' is resolved to have a permanent settlement on the moon by 2043. A good number of political figures have very grand ambitions but this, I feel, exceeds even the grandest of them. I note with a degree of amusement that, as a sign of his political versatility, he went on to announce that he intended to be a keynote speaker at a UKIP conference.

These rather eccentric aspects of his ambitions were unknown to me until a while ago. I did know, as does everyone, that he had relationships with one of The Cheeky Girls and with Welsh weather reporter Sian Lloyd. Both relationships lasted a little while but my

131

dealings with him were quite brief. He discovered that I was going out to Estonia to try and promote further trade deals between that country and Wales. He asked if he could accompany me. I said no.

One of the jobs one had as a BBC governor was to attend the party conferences for the three major political parties. This obviously was something of a time commitment, but it was felt at the BBC that our impartiality would be visibly stressed by our appearance at these events. Some of these conferences I enjoyed; others were rather more tiresome. A regular at many conferences held by the Labour Party was Paul Flynn.

Paul Flynn was a good man. He was a man prepared to scrutinise, not just observe, and he looked into matters with intelligence and perspicuity, whereas it is a sad fact that some politicians cannot see past their party's manifesto. I am sure that many politicians enter the public arena with the intention of doing good. As they say though, power corrupts and absolute power rots the soul.

I was very interested in doing something about the suicide rate, both within Wales and across the UK. My interest in trying to do something about poisonings had led to my development of Carbomix, the charcoal substance I have mentioned in Chapter 7. Subsequent to that I developed a paracetamol tablet that was fool proof in terms of preventing suicide by paracetamol. The analgesic power worked normally but the composition of the tablets was such that one could not kill oneself by taking them, no matter how many one took. Paul Flynn, a fellow North Walian, was impressed by this work, especially as it was being done by a small firm in Tredegar, in defiance of the major multinational pharmaceutical companies.

My argument was that paracetamol could be bought anywhere, in a local filling station say, and this ready availability meant that people were likely to assume that there could be little harm in the tablets. There is a phenomenon known as parasuicide, which refers to people, and young people mainly, who do not really intend to kill themselves, but want to draw attention to their emotional and/or psychological state. These people rarely realise that as few as fifteen or sixteen tablets is enough to cause death. And the death is not the peaceful passing that they might imagine, but an agonising one caused by organ failure.

I discovered that if you mix the amino acid methionine, which is as cheap as chips, if not cheaper, with paracetamol, a hepatoprotective chemical reaction takes place. That is to say, it protects the liver from the potentially damaging effects of paracetamol.

The makers of branded paracetamol tablets were not interested in making this safe form of paracetamol. Production costs were not the issue; it was a matter of perception. Changing the tablets might lead potential customers to think that the company's product hitherto had been unsafe. It might even lead to litigation.

Paul Flynn was, like me. a supporter of the Welsh football team. As far as club football is concerned, I have always been a supporter of Liverpool FC. As one might expect, coming from North Wales I grew up supporting Wrexham, but it is not always inspiring to be a fan of a lower league or non-league football club. I have not been placed in the awkward situation where I was forced to watch my two teams competing against each other - Wrexham and Liverpool have only met three times in official competitions - so there has been no conflict of interest for me. Latterly I came to have a fondness for Swansea City too. I actually awarded Swansea Chairman Huw Jenkins his honorary PhD whilst I was on the university council. Getting Swansea into the premier league was a great achievement and significant as far as the university was concerned, since it put the city and its university firmly on the map, so to speak. Incidentally, I had the pleasure of awarding a similar honour to Welsh actress Ruth Madoc too. I found her warmth and humour delightful.

Speaking of honours, I should mention the ceremony I attended in Buckingham Palace in 2005, where I was knighted by perhaps the world's most famous leader, Her Majesty Queen Elizabeth II. I have said that I gave Ed Balls and Peter Hain a helping nudge, and they were kind enough to put my name forward for a knighthood. It was a particularly proud occasion for my mother, I think, for she attended too, along with my wife Ann and my two children.

For anyone aspiring to become a knight of the realm I should proffer a little warning that the occasion does have its expenses. I bought myself a new morning coat and new outfits for the rest of my family, and I also purchased the official VHS video recording of the event, though I admit I now have no idea where that ancient piece of technology is gathering dust. We engaged a driver to take us up to London too. Someone asked me once why I was not put off by the thought of having to drive from Brecon to the palace and back in a day, but my driving experiences in Nigeria, where a thousand-mile trip was a fairly commonplace experience, must have hardened me to long journeys. I was also used to driving from Leighton Buzzard to Brecon two or three times a week for years, of course.

I had never turned up for my own degree ceremonies. Inverted snobbery perhaps. I came to realise, however, that you are not doing it for your own sake, but for the sake of your loved ones. I had denied my parents this vicarious thrill and my father had died before my knighthood ceremony, so I was happy to see my mother enjoying the reflected glory of the Buckingham Palace event. I also at last attended a degree awards ceremony when I was awarded an honorary Doctor of Science degree from The University of Wales.

The process of receiving an honour at Buckingham Palace involves being taken to a kind of holding pen, where you are briefed on what to do and what to say to the queen. There are very strict protocols about this sort of thing. Then you are called forward and taken into the main room. You kneel on a footstool and the monarch taps you on the shoulders with her ceremonial sword and thanks you for your services. Frankly, it is something of a rigmarole, but I know my mother was enthralled by it. I think she was proud too of my academic and professional qualifications. Occasionally I have to list my post-nominals, which include a Fellowship of the Royal Pharmaceutical Society as well as my two degrees and my OBE, but, as is evident from the title page of this book, I prefer to be known simply as Roger Jones.

Not quite as famous as our queen, but certainly a very important world leader at the time I met him, was Deng Xiaoping, the Chairman of the Chinese Communist Party and de facto president of

China. While I was working at Wellcome we were manufacturing a vaccine for foot and mouth disease, a condition debilitating to the agricultural industry. China, in particular, had huge problems with the disease. If they had been able to control it, they could have doubled their pork production, which is a major element of their food industry. The idea was that we would sell them a vaccination plant and the technology required for vaccine production. Franchising was not considered an option because it was felt that we would have no real control over affairs if we pursued that route.

We were ultimately unsuccessful in persuading the Chinese to accept the deal because Deng Xiaoping could not admit to the prevalence of foot and mouth disease in his country because his predecessor Mao Tse Tung, or Mao Zedong as he is now commonly known, had decreed that there was no foot and mouth disease in China. Mao is a legend, of course, and his utterances were seemingly sacrosanct.

We had arranged for a team to be at railway sidings in Hong Kong, where experts would take blood samples from pigs being transported from China. There are different strains of the disease, as we have seen in other diseases such as Covid-19, and our results were able to show us clearly in which region in China the pigs had contracted it. Thus, we were able to map a vaccination programme which could offer different treatments according to the individual strains. It was clever stuff, but face-saving apparently trumped medical innovation in the China of that time.

Chapter 11 *At Peace in Battle*

Sure, I could retire any time. I don't need to work for money. But retire to what? I love fishing and I go every time I get a chance. But a man with pride in his profession needs to work

Van Heflin

I have lived in a village called Battle, four miles from Brecon, for the last thirty odd years. Actually, my house is called Battle House, something that is immediately made evident to visitors because the name is carved into the stone entrance to the property. It's an interesting name because we are a couple of hundred miles away from the scene of the famous battle that took place in 1066. That conflict of course came to be known as the Battle of Hastings, which might seem slightly odd, in that Hastings was seven miles away from the battlefield, and there were other villages and settlements closer to the scene of the conflict. We have the Domesday Book to thank for the name, it appears.

The village where I live came to be called Battle, just as Battle in Sussex received its name, because it was the scene of conflict between a Norman invader and the indigenous people. In the case of Breconshire's Battle, it was not a William but a Bernard who was waging war. Harold's forces succumbed to the Normans within a day; Welsh princes were made of sterner stuff apparently and withstood the foreign invasion for some time. Eventually Bernard de Neufmarché, or Bernard Newmarch, as he came to be known, was sent on a sort of 'mopping up' operation to overcome the Welsh forces. He made a vow that he would give the land on which the battle was fought to his god if he were to prove victorious. He was, needless to say, because Norman warriors were technologically far superior, and Bernard was true to his word. He gave the land to God, or rather, to some of his servants, in the form of some Norman abbots in Sussex. They sent a group of brothers to Wales to farm the area, although they did not choose to consecrate the land and build an abbey on the land here. Instead, they simply erected a few buildings as houses, barns and stables and so forth. Fascinatingly, in 1976, when there was a very hot dry summer, the outline of these buildings was revealed.

In about 1760, although I cannot be precise about the exact year, a man called Henry Mitchell turned up. He was very rich, for this was the time when people amassed great wealth in Britain because of trade, and in particular trade through the East India Company. I am uncertain whether he was a businessman or an officer in the army, but it is evident that he wanted to establish an estate somewhere in the country. A number of his *confrères* had travelled to Ireland to set up their great estates there, and it is thought he was of a similar mind. Perhaps he was exhausted or saddle sore from his travels, however. Assuredly anyway, he never made it to Ireland. He built what is now my home and it was dubbed 'Mr Mitchell's New House.'

I have gleaned what I know about the history of Battle House largely from a work by a man called Theophilus Jones, who was a solicitor in Brecon in the eighteenth century. After he retired from that profession, he became a local historian of the county. He mentions how the house came to be built in his *History of the County of Brecknockshire*. I am extremely lucky to own a very rare copy of this two-volume tome, the copy that was given to Jones's amanuensis. The books are the size of concrete blocks, and not far off the weight of them either. I have waded through some of the text, but it is not an easy read. Amongst less controversial musings, Jones propagates an alarming theory that it is unwise to teach boys to read, because it leads to them misapprehending the Bible, to be given to incessant prating and to generally be likely to encourage them to cause trouble. All I can say is that I guess it is just as well Jones's book is out of print.

Battle House is a stone built Georgian edifice on three floors, with a huge basement. There are four reception rooms and the upper floors both have four bedrooms. Naturally, it was not designed with modern notions of personal hygiene in mind, having but a single bathroom for all the house's occupants. Ann and I readily agreed that we needed to install a number of ensuite bathrooms as soon as we moved in. Fortunately, our house had missed the attentions of those people who were set on 'improving' everything they got their hands on, the Victorians. Accordingly, the house still retains its Georgian character.

The whole of the basement area was taken up by work areas for the servants. There was a laundry, a bakery, a brewery, an extensive vaulted wine cellar and an area for meat-salting. In addition, there was a communal area, or mess, where the servants could congregate. There was no sleeping accommodation in the house for this underclass; they would have slept in barns or outhouses on the estate. I have kept the wine cellar, because I think such a facility is highly desirable if one can afford to stock it, but I have converted one of the other rooms for use as an office. Some of the basement area is also taken up with my large collection of books. I will elaborate on my library in a short while.

We were very fortunate to find Battle House on the market when we were looking to move from Berkhamsted. A local doctor was living in the house when we bought it, but little money had been spent on the place for a long time. It meant that we would have to invest a considerable sum, but Ann, in particular, could see huge potential for improvement. Luckily, it seemed that along with this find she must have discovered that money tree I mentioned earlier, for we did spend an inordinate amount on renovations.

It was not simply that we had found an ideal home for ourselves, however. I had been researching locations where we could send our children Hefin and Bryony to good schools without them having to board. Both children had gone to private preparatory school and Bryony had just sat her 'O' levels in Berkhamsted School. As I remarked earlier, we needed to find somewhere that would give her the sixth form education she needed to prosper at university, enter a good profession and thrive in later life.

There was basically a choice of three schools in South Wales that met my criteria – the single sex Monmouth independent schools, Christ College in Brecon, and Llandovery College. All are expensive - eighteen to twenty thousand pounds per annum at current rates - but money was not so much the issue. After all, I had been paying fees at Berkhamsted. What spurred me most was my desire for my son and daughter to live at home and not have to travel enormous distances to school. I decided that if we lived in Monmouth I would be too far away from my work in Tredegar. It was even further from Llandovery. Ultimately, I decided that choice of school would have to depend on where we found a house that was suitable to our needs.

In those days Christ College was not considered to be one of the finest educational establishments in the country. It was rather a scruffy place, I felt, and clearly was to be viewed as the sort of place to send one's sons if one was a farmer. By contrast, Llandovery catered more for the sons of the clergy. It also had a much more Welsh ethos. Teaching was through the medium of English, but it was less Anglophile than Christ College, where Welsh language and culture were almost excluded from the curriculum. Perhaps because of this Hefin is not a very confident Welsh speaker. He does understand the language, but he prefers to converse in English. This is just as well, you might say, for he lives in Canada right now!

On the other hand, his sister Bryony speaks Welsh fluently. This might seem surprising, because much of Bryony's education took place in the quintessentially English home counties. She was, however. fortunate in that she was able to spend long summer holidays on the farm in Montgomeryshire where her grandmother, her *nain,* lived. Since she and her uncle were by choice monoglot Welsh speakers, Bryony enjoyed almost total immersion in the language, you might say. I do not think Hefin regrets not having the same fluency; he retains a firm sense of his Celtic identity, a fact which is affirmed by his choice of name for his daughter, Cerys. I am pleased to say that both he and Bryony have given their children Welsh names, Cerys in Hefin's case and Tomos and Aneira in

Bryony's case. I will say more about the value I place on my Welsh identity and heritage in due course.

I think both of my children enjoyed their time at Christ College, though they might occasionally have felt subsequently that they could have stood a better chance of an Oxbridge education if they had gone to a more prestigious establishment. Perhaps I am being unfair here. They both went to Imperial College in London, and I am absolutely certain that they received a first-class education there. Perhaps a better education than they might have had in some of the Oxford and Cambridge colleges, especially since they were not pursuing a degree in Classics or PPE, but undertaking courses in medicine. Nevertheless, whatever one feels about it, the cachet of an Oxbridge education, plus the inevitable network of influential friends and associates that can be formed at a famous old college, remain highly valuable commodities for the ambitious young man or woman in Britain today.

I, for one, wish I had had the opportunity to go to Oxbridge. And I sometimes wonder whether Ann and I could have pushed our children harder, but I suspect that Christ College did not do its full part in raising expectations either. Bryony had top grades in all of her 'A' level subjects and Hefin did very well too, though he did not work as hard as his sister. He had a Damascene revelation, one might say, and applied himself seriously once at university. He now works as a radiologist. Bryony is a very successful obstetrician.

I have to say I did not see enough of my children while they were growing up, because of the pressures of my work. Probably, and this might seem ironic, I saw more of them when we were living in Berkhamsted. This was because I drove them to school each morning. The twenty-five-minute journey was always taken up with mental games, scientific discussions and problem-solving. I like to believe that these mobile seminars must have encouraged them to think for themselves more, rather than just passively absorb the received wisdom of their teachers.

Hefin was ten years old when we moved to Battle so we decided to enrol him at the local primary school in order for him to get to know some local people before he went to Christ College. Perhaps this was helpful; at any rate he became a very gregarious young man, interested in sport and a capable player at both rugby and football. He was a very good rugby centre in his schooldays. It is even possible that his rugby skills helped with his application to Imperial College. He thought he would excel at rugby there too, but sometimes reality has a frightening way of dashing your dreams. And the reality was that he was six foot two but only weighed about twelve stone soaking wet. He thought he was a fast runner, but he found himself coming up against opposition centres who were equally fast, or faster, and weighed sixteen stone. He endeavoured to gain weight in the way that young people do these days, going to the gym and devouring protein shakes, but he only made it to about fourteen stone. He reasoned that he stood a good chance of getting hurt if he continued playing rugby, and he made the correct decision, in my view, to switch to the relatively less dangerous position of a midfield general in association football.

As I remarked, I found that I was seeing less of my children now we were living in Battle because I was spending so much time in my factory and laboratory in Tredegar. Perhaps rather playfully, I offered to give that responsibility up and get a nine to five job working in a Boots pharmacy, but no one believed I would actually do that. Obviously, the huge difference in income that this would have entailed was a significant issue, but, as I think Ann and my children realised, it was not only about money. I wanted a measure of control. I was always rather of a mind with Simon and Garfunkel in preferring to be a hammer than a nail.

My mother was a big influence on me in terms of my attitude to my new life in Battle. And by that I mean that she had a sort of negative influence. She was exceptionally bright - few women of her generation entered higher education, as she did - but she set her targets very low, and she tried to imbue in me a similar modesty of ambition. I reacted against this and sided more with my father, who wanted me to succeed through my intelligence, but also to realise that it was not just intelligence or knowledge, but the application of that knowledge that was the key to success. He was content to accept a fairly humble station as far as his own work was concerned, but he wanted more for his family. I must have inherited this drive, I guess. I hope and believe I have passed on that ambition and drive to my children.

The importance of family was something I have always endeavoured to stress. Though Bryony and Hefin both have partners and their own families, they are still very close, despite there being a six-year gap between them. They are in constant touch with each other and with me and Ann. Indeed, Hefin flew over from Canada recently, specially to celebrate Bryony's 'big' birthday.

I miss seeing Hefin, his wife Susie and their daughter Cerys on a more regular basis than living on opposite sides of the Atlantic allows, of course. Nevertheless, I completely understood my son's motives in moving abroad. Having had his epiphany about the need to work harder at university than he had at school, Hefin applied himself with admirable diligence in his studies. When I observed how he went about his studies as a youngster I felt that he if he got 51% in an exam, he would rue the extra effort he had put in to get that 1%, when 50% would have sufficed for a pass mark. Later he aimed much higher of course and he duly qualified as a radiologist.

He could have found work anywhere as a consultant, but he was disillusioned about the state of the NHS and decided to go to Edmonton in Canada, where his expertise was very much in demand. What had happened was that a number of physicians who had been working at Harefield Hospital had developed a way of interpreting the scar tissue that is left after a patient has had a heart attack. It was ground-breaking science and much in demand in other parts of the world. A number of the team who had worked on the project, discovering how to interpret the scar tissue and therefore how to develop prognoses and treatments, decided to emigrate to Canada. Hefin was headhunted by these medics, who were by this stage considering retirement and the opportunity to live off their ill-gotten gains. Of course, I mean well-gotten gains, given their important work. As a result, they were looking to recruit new talent. Needless to say, the remuneration was far in excess of the salary he could have achieved in the UK working in the public sector. Also, and I am a little sad to say this, both working conditions and professional expectations are much higher for Hefin in Canada than he experienced in Britain.

I am happy for him because he is doing important work and his wife is able to bring up Cerys without having to think about having to go out to work to supplement the family's income. Without wishing to sound too proud, I can say that he earns enough to provide for his family, and provide very well indeed. And there is always a flat at Battle House for them when they come to the UK. I am comforted by the fact that they have the wherewithal, and the time, to bring Cerys over to see her doting grandparents a few times a year.

I am proud too that my daughter has grasped the importance of excellence in her field of medicine. As I have stated, she is an obstetrician. She trained in London and also in Australia, where she was working alongside some excellent practitioners and educators. She went out to Australia to gain some experience abroad before it was time to start in earnest on a professional career in Britain, and perhaps meet a potential husband and settle down. Ann's last words before she went on her travels were, 'Do have a good time but please don't fall in love with an Australian.'

She promptly fell in love with an Australian, our son-in-law Nick, but fortunately she was able to persuade him to come to the UK. This might have caused Nick's parents some chagrin, but it delighted us. Now she delivers babies for a living, and this must be a fine way to earn a living. Better than driving back and forth across Nigeria, or even back and forth between Berkhamsted and Tredegar, anyway. She mainly deals with private patients, who are prepared to pay considerable sums of money for such care, but she also works for the NHS at Queen Charlotte's Hospital in London. She and Nick live in Chiswick, but they have recently bought another home in Saundersfoot. They love West Wales. What is there not to love in this part of God's country? They were looking for somewhere near a beach and have been fortunate enough to find an ideal home. Like the great Welsh poet R S Thomas, I am not a great supporter of Welsh second homes for non-natives, but I find it hard to argue against having a second home in such a beautiful place for Welsh people who have to work in big cities like London.

Nick is an Intensive Care specialist in St Thomas' Hospital in Westminster, and he is a top man in his field. Between them Bryony and Nick earn a very healthy amount and are able to provide a good living for their family. I am saying that medicine pays well, but in truth there are prohibitive costs involved in terms of the insurance cover that doctors often have to provide for themselves. This is particularly the case for obstetricians, because statistically they are the most likely figures to incur legal costs in cases of litigation.

We see Bryony and Nick's children, Tomos and Aneira, quite regularly. Tomos attends St Paul's school and is a lovely gentle soul. Aneira is a budding sportswoman who loves horse riding and playing rugby, which she does for her school. She attends a private school too. I have been assured that this is the best education for my grandchildren, as I was convinced it was for my children. I say this because I think such schooling provides a more rounded cultural experience than the more limited education I received myself in a state school. When, as a young man, I first picked up a *Times* crossword, for instance, I was horrified at the realisation that there were so many gaps in my knowledge. The same thing applied when I joined the Board of Governors at the BBC. People threw around cultural references I had never heard of. Nobody ever said anything about *Peer Gynt* or *The Doll's House* back in Bala. I could decline a noun and conjugate a verb in Latin, but apparently there was more to a broad education than the dubious benefits of such rote learning.

I know lots of people think that the existence of elitist establishments like public schools is an anachronism in modern society. The Labour party considers, for instance, that taxation for such schools should be reviewed. In my opinion we should be levelling society, but levelling up rather than down. Taxation is always a thorny issue, of course. Nobody wants to give up a significant portion of their income. At one stage, a long time ago now admittedly, the rich were being taxed at a rate of 83% on the highest part of their earnings. It did not raise huge amounts of money for public expenditure, but it did drive out high achievers in what came to be called the 'brain drain'.

You have to be realistic. Self-interest will always be a major factor in the way that people choose to vote. Once you are assured that you can provide for yourself and your family in a way that fairly reflects your efforts, then altruism can also be an important factor. Though I am no fan of Conservative politicians these days, I do think people should pay their way for such things as education and healthcare, if they can afford to do so. People argue that we are not all equal in terms of skill and intelligence. and therefore we should take care of those who cannot earn enough to pay for a private service in these fields. My response is that I am not my brother's keeper. Having said that, I also believe if we do not have compassion, we are nothing. I have never said I was not made up of contradictions!

We may need more policemen, which is another Conservative mantra, but I think even more important is the need for better training. I am not even against such practices as 'stop and search', but there has to be meticulous monitoring of any such potential infringements on civil liberties. I run the risk, I realise, of being regarded as some sort of racist when I claim that certain sections of society are to be viewed as more likely to offend. What I would say, however, is that we need to ensure that everyone in our society needs to be integrated into a common value system. This means better education and better, more efficient, and less self-serving government. I can live with some aspects of Tory policies, but other aspects are abhorrent to me. Some recent suggestions, such as the deportation of illegal immigrants to Rwanda, I find completely unworkable. I know Rwanda well; I still have a factory in that country. It is a dangerous place, often threatened by corruption. Aside from any moral objections one might have about such a policy, I believe immigrants would soon bribe their way out of Africa and make their way back to the UK. It is pretty evident that the policy was flagged up purely as a piece of propaganda anyway, a warning to potential illegal immigrants, rather than a real solution to the problem of people trying to get to Britain in inflatable boats.

I was asked not long ago who it was that I regarded as of any substance in the current crop of politicians. I struggled to think of any I admired. William Hague was perhaps a man capable of honesty, but I cannot think that Jeremy Hunt, Dominic Raab, or, sadly, any of the women striving for power in present times offer very much. Liz Truss was always doomed to fail, I thought. She struck me as a type known in the nineties as a 'ladette'. Jacob Rees-Mogg, the member of parliament for the eighteenth century, as one wag called him, was a self-creation. A self-parody even. Pince-nez spectacles, my foot! I did feel at one point that Matt Hancock might be a man who could bring some focus to whatever ministry he ended up leading, but plainly he needed to sort out his personal life first. At the time I am writing he has announced that he intends to join the cast of 'celebrities' participating in the TV show *I'm a Celebrity ... Get Me Out of Here*. I think this speaks volumes about his loss of faith in his political career prospects. In the interest of impartiality, I should say that I am not deeply impressed by the present complement of Labour politicians either. I simply cannot see a great deal of charisma or talent; it is mainly noise that I hear.

At the risk of sounding polemical I must say that I think Boris Johnson was the cause of much unhappiness in Britain. He does not take himself seriously and he certainly does not take running a country seriously. I always saw him as an entertainer, but not even an entertainer with a set of admirable skills. He is no conjuror or trapeze artist, despite his comical zipwire antics. To me he is more a ringmaster for a series of clowns. The country deserves better.

David Cameron, of course, was partly to blame for the mess we now find ourselves in. The Labour Party had created something of a cult figure in Tony Blair and the Tory response was to create a figure of their own, who was adept at the same sort of PR, who fitted the right age profile and who apparently had a similar energy about him. In trying to deal with his own backbenchers, Cameron painted himself into a corner over the Brexit referendum. Seemingly he never thought that people would be short-sighted or insular enough in their outlook to vote to leave the European Union. I saw no advantages for me in Brexit, as a businessman or as a British citizen. For me it was a pure waste of time, effort and money.

What is clear to me is that it behoves us to respect those politicians who genuinely try to improve the lives of their constituents, irrespective of their party allegiance. If ever I see TV coverage of debates in the House of Commons it is the MPs who are urging action to meet the needs of their local area, rather than those who are trying to impress with their wordplay and soundbites that I warm to. 'Warm'; is a strong word, nevertheless.

Before I was inveigled into this diatribe, or before I inveigled myself into it, I should say, I was pointing out that we had found a good place to live and a school where our children could do well if they exerted themselves. It was then time to turn our attention to our immediate surroundings. Ann has always been very interested in gardening and she set to the task of designing and planting what is now a considerable series of gardens. Fourteen acres in all, I believe.

There were no lawns as such when we moved in. There was a fair amount of land, but it was uncultivated. We brought in earth moving equipment and expended a lot of effort terracing the land at the back of the house for lawns and shrubberies. Unfortunately, the land which is at the front of the house was not included in the sale when we bought Battle House. Previous owners had sold it off. As parcels came back onto the market, however, I bought them and restored the land as gardens. Actually, the property now is situated within a hundred and sixty acres of its own land. Much of this is leased out to farmers for use as pastureland, of course.

I had originally thought to develop a small shooting estate. For this you need the right sort of topography, and trees would need to be planted for cover. That ambition was never properly fulfilled but I can say that we have arrived at a stage where the house and gardens satisfy us both. There is room to wander about; our dogs do not need to be transported to somewhere else for their walks, and we can sit outside in complete privacy and enjoy our wonderful views of the Brecon hills.

I have also installed two ponds. They are a couple of acres each and I have stocked them with trout. It is very pleasant to come home on a summer's evening and amble down to one of these ponds, rod in hand and heart on high. I do not kill my catch. They live to fight another day.

Chapter 12   *Leisure? What's That?*

There are always new places to go fishing. For any fisherman, there's always a new place, always a new horizon

Jack Nicklaus

I have not retired. I still work in two companies - BioExtractions Wales, which is sited in Tredegar, and Phytovation, which is based in Caernarfon. I also have a company called Suprex on my Caernarfon site, which uses super-critical carbon dioxide for extraction of molecules from substrates. The processes involved are massively high-tech because pressures are 300 bar plus. Carbon dioxide is unique in that it can either be a polar solvent, like water or alcohol, or it can be oily solvent. What determines which category it fits into is the pressure it is put under. Hence, we can extract and release a target chemical. I believe as far as the whole of the UK is concerned, we have the best equipment and the best skills to utilise that equipment for the extraction of chemicals from plants. What we are doing is providing development opportunities for companies who might want to extract chemicals economically from their materials. An example would be the extraction of alcohol from beer to create non-alcoholic beer. Supercritical carbon dioxide is the key to this operation. As it is for the extraction of caffeine for caffeine-free coffee.

I do not have a great deal of leisure time because these companies take up a fair amount of my time. Typically, I will phone the people working at these companies first thing in the morning, then twice or three times a week I will visit the plant. I am in my eightieth year, but I cannot even imagine not working. Also, I like to use my non-working time fruitfully. That can mean fishing or shooting, of course, but I do also ensure that I find time to read. Usually, I will read a book a week. I think it is one of life's great pleasures, sitting in a comfortable chair reading a good book.

At the time of writing this memoir I am halfway through a book by Jan Morris called *The Matter of Wales*. I have already mentioned that my son-in-law and daughter have bought a house in Saundersfoot. The house is a lovely old listed building called The Priory, but they were fortunate enough to be able to buy the contents of the house as well. Amongst the books that were included in this sale was a hardback edition of this book by Jan Morris, a riveting account of the history of Wales. I borrowed it from them when I first went to the house, on the occasion of Bryony's birthday celebration in October 2022. Subsequently I discovered that I already possessed a paperback copy! I am not, however, one of those people whose house is stacked with books on the 'Books I Intend To Read One Day' list. Of the thirty thousand odd books on my shelves, I would venture to say I have read a high proportion of them.

It is an eclectic collection. A glance at the bookshelves in my drawing room would show Peter Jukes' *Fall of the House of Murdoch* next to Bruce Chatwin's *On the Black Hill* and William Boyd's *The Blue Afternoon* next to John Keegan's *The First World War* and David Attenborough's *The Life of Birds*. There is a book devoted to microbes, Peter Garrett's *The Coming Plague*, and there is a volume by Desmond Hamill that deals with the army in Northern Ireland, provocatively entitled *Pig in the Middle*. I will read about politics, history, war, adventure (I would recommend Ranulph Fiennes' *Mind Over Matter* for a portrayal of man's fortitude against the elements). I do not have a single favourite author, though I have read lots of certain writers' works. Actually, I would say that of the thirty thousand books that I own, about three thousand are about fishing! As I have hinted above, I enjoy reading histories, particularly military histories, but I like to read biographies and fiction as well, of course.

Sometimes my interests overlap. I read *The Old Man and the*

Sea by Earnest Hemingway, for example, both for its literary merits and for its account of a battle between a man and a mighty fish. *Moby Dick* is a better book, however. I also read Hemingway's *For Whom the Bell Tolls.*, where Hemingway's hero is embroiled in the Spanish Civil War. I was interested in the factual accounts of the war as well as the destiny of the characters. I think literary critics nowadays are less impressed by some of Hemingway's macho instincts and I admit I have not thought about him for some time.

I loved the literature produced during Britain's colonial times. Kipling was a favourite author of mine and I read E. M. Forster's novels too. Anything to do with the Raj was fascinating for me. Of course, I was not in India during this heyday of British imperial might, but I did experience a kind of echo of it in my time in Nigeria, as I have described earlier.

I have always enjoyed reading what is classed as 'literature', even though I did not do 'A' level English. I consumed works such as Dickens' novels without the sort of reservations that many people have in present times about wordiness or length. I read some of the great Russian classics, like *Crime and Punishment* and *War and Peace* too. Tolstoy's masterpiece took me some time, I will admit, because I found I could only read a few pages every day. The book was very dense and complex but ultimately it was well worth the effort. Again, as well as the human drama, there are interesting observations on the strategies of warfare by Napoleon and his generals. I appreciate writers who can offer sweeping accounts of society. Possibly for this reason I have recently immersed myself in the world of Antony Trollope's *Barsetshire Chronicles.*

As I was reaching early manhood in the nineteen sixties there was a slew of so-called social realist novels, including books like *Room at the Top* and *The Loneliness of the Long-Distance Runner*. I very much enjoyed these newer voices speaking to me about a more provincial and working-class life than the novels of the nineteenth century. It being the nineteen sixties, I also read Jean-Paul Sartre, whose existentialist thinking was a compelling alternative to the more staid convictions of our elders, for idealistic young men and women. Books like *L'Être et le néant* and *La Nausée* were *de rigeur* for undergraduates at that time. Some of us talked about the books; some of us actually read them.

I have a lot of military books because I have a fascination with the conduct of war and the strategies devised by successful generals. As has been the case so often in my life, the question 'Why?' intrigued me when I read about military campaigns. Operation Barbarossa, for instance, stands as one of the most catastrophical campaigns of any war, but certainly of World War Two. The plan to conquer and subdue Russia which Hitler carried out in 1941 was highly flawed in a number of respects, but mainly because Hitler underestimated the resilience of the Soviet forces and the debilitating effects of a bitterly cold winter climate in Russia. We have seen almost the same underestimation, this time by Russian leaders, with regard to their 'special operation' in Ukraine. Sheer brute strength is not an adequate substitute for tactical wisdom.

This might be a mantra for business too, which might be seen in some ways as analogous to war. In both spheres one needs to discover and deploy strategies to overcome competitors. Outmanoeuvring rivals or opponents is part of the game.

I was drawn into William Boyd's *An Ice Cream War* because of the writer's connections with Africa, but also because of the interesting reflections on war in that novel. It might not seem so at first, but the book is very humorous, and a biting satire on the incompetence of the military leaders who thought that the First World War would not last for more than a couple of months. Boyd got the title for his work from a letter written by an English Lieutenant-Colonel, who said that the armies could not fight for any extended period of time in East Africa because 'we would melt like ice cream in the sun'. I was strongly reminded of this sort of hubris by some of the people I met in the world of business and in political situations.

I possess, as many people do, a copy of *The Complete Plays of Shakespeare*. I am not sure if a majority of owners have ever done much more than dip into the treasures therein, however. I have to say I have read a lot of Shakespeare. It might seem an odd reason, but I have been spurred into this reading because I love to do *The Times* crossword and compilers are rather fond of Shakespearian references in their clues. Sometimes I have been drawn into reading a whole play, or at least a substantial part of one, in my chasing down a solution to one of these clues. I do not suppose people read *Cymbeline* or *Timon of Athens* much these days, but erudite crossword compilers have found a way to seduce people like me into attempting to tackle them!

I have not seen all of Shakespeare's plays, but I did enjoy school visits to Stratford-upon-Avon. I have also watched a good number of the plays on television of course. The BBC undertook a massive project in the nineteen seventies and eighties to produce all thirty-seven of Shakespeare's plays over a seven-year period. Interestingly, it was Glamis Castle which excited the series producer Cedric Messina as a setting for his planned *As You Like It*. I once stayed at this castle on a shooting trip to Scotland. Messina then envisioned producing the entire oeuvre for TV, though he met with some considerable opposition. The very creative and brilliant Jonathon Miller took over from Series Three onwards, and I think the enterprise was an excellent one, typical of the BBC as a corporation at the time.

I have my favourites amongst Shakespeare's plays, perhaps particularly the tragedies. Someone once asked me who I would cast myself as if I were to be a Shakespearian character. I immediately thought of Macbeth. Not Julius Caesar definitely. Maybe a touch of Autolycus though, that 'snapper-up of unconsidered trifles' in *A Winter's Tale*, though actually it was bigger fish I often went after, of course.

When I worked at the BBC governors would be given a pack of, say, ten BBC publications at Christmas. These might include some light-hearted books, which would leaven the weight of the more serious books I quite often tackled.

I would not class myself as a connoisseur of paintings, but I do appreciate art too. Kyffin Williams is a favourite painter of mine. He was knighted for his contribution to the visual arts, and he is almost certainly Wales's most famous artist. I have one of his landscapes in the drawing room at Battle House. It is dark and rather severe, but I

152

think it captures the majestic topography of his native Gwynedd superbly.

I did not go to the theatre as much as I should have, I think now, whilst I was living near London. I did have the privilege of seeing my daughter Bryony on stage while she was at Imperial College, however. She played Eliza Doolittle in *My Fair Lady,* and she acted in a number of other university productions too. Indeed, acting would have been her first choice of career if I had not succeeded in persuading her to concentrate on following a medical path. She trained as a gynaecologist and obstetrician but has focused on the obstetric side of things for most of her career. Perhaps her natural ability to assume a part has helped her in her dealings with patients.

Although I rarely go to see plays anymore, I sometimes go to see Welsh National Opera productions in Cardiff. I suppose, like most people, these days I derive most of my cultural pleasure from watching television. I enjoy watching wildlife documentaries particularly. I enjoy a good film too. A genre I like a lot is The Western., particularly classics like *High Noon, The Searchers,* and John Wayne movies like *Stagecoach, Red River, The Alamo* and *The Man Who Shot Liberty Valance.* I thought *The Good, the Bad and the Ugly* was a brilliant new take on the genre too. In contrast to the dusty realism of Serge Leone's masterpiece, I really enjoy the Bond films for their silliness, make believe and high-octane drama. I was rather fond of James Bond's Aston Martin; so much so that I bought one for Ann, though this car is a high performance four-door Rapide, not the classic DB5. This is the car that bears the numberplate 5RJ. We take it out occasionally, partly to enjoy listening to the throaty growl of the six-litre engine, but it is usually ensconced safely in one of my garages at Battle House.

I do not watch a lot of television drama these days, but I have old favourites that I rewatch often. *Only Fools and Horses* and *M*A*S*H* are two series I can go back to at any time. I like the juxtaposition of the comic and the serious in the latter. 'Suicide is painless; it brings on many changes', the lyric to the theme tune of *M*A*S*H,* is a perfect demonstration of this sort of absurdity.

The dramas I enjoyed in the past include Dennis Potter plays like *Pennies from Heaven, The Singing Detective* and *Blue Remembered Hills*. I was also influenced, I think, by Potter's early work *Vote, Vote for Nigel Barton*. It was a play that dealt with class and politics in ways that touched my own life, since I identified with Potter as a man from a fairly modest background who finds himself thrust into a very different world. In Potter's case it was the privileged world of Oxford University. The central character Barton, a fairly autobiographical version of the playwright, then becomes disillusioned by the compromises of political electioneering. In my case, as I hope I have shown so far, it was finding myself dealing with powerful and often privileged men and then having to find ways to combat incompetence, corruption and compromise in both the world of industry and the public domain.

I go to the Hay Festival of Literature every year. Sometimes I attend talks given by journalists and pundits, simply to put a face to the name of someone whose articles I read perhaps. My newspaper of choice is *The Times*, which I read every day. I need serious news coverage, but I also love the sardonic and satirical glance at the news that you get from *Private Eye,* which I look forward to reading when it is delivered every fortnight. I am a regular watcher of *Have I Got News for You* too, because it is great fun watching self-important public figures being lampooned and brought down to earth by witty commentators. There is something of Ian Hislop in me, I feel, but perhaps also something of the brasher, less pompous Paul Merton too. At least I hope so. I mentioned in the last chapter that I regarded Liz Truss as something of a 'ladette'. It was *Private Eye*, I recall, who coined this term for her, because of the way the journalists there viewed her as someone who tried to ingratiate herself with men by aping their behaviour. It did her little good.

Also a real treat when it arrives at my door is *The Field*, which gives me my regular fix of news and views about country matters and the sports of hunting and fishing so close to my heart.

Thinking about culture in our country today there are terms I do not understand. 'Woke' is an alien word to me. Recently I heard a government minister using the word as an accusation, along with the phrases 'Tofu-eating' and '*Guardian*-reading' as terms of deprecation. As I say, I read *The Times*, but my son Hefin is an avid *Guardian* reader. He claims that he refuses to be in the same room as anyone who reads *The Daily Mail*. In some ways that might seem unfortunate, because his mother Ann is something of a fan of that organ, but only for the puzzles in the centre pages, she insists. I cannot endorse any of the attitudes of *The Daily Mail* or *The Daily Telegraph*, though I do like the crossword puzzle in *The Daily Telegraph*.

There are certain authors whose names or works feature in the crossword puzzles I like to try and solve. Naturally, these tend to be older novels and older writers, like Trollope, whom I mentioned just now. But I do not read purely for the satisfaction of garnering solutions to crosswords, needless to say. I enjoy the escapism of writers like Ian Fleming, but I also derived a lot of interest from my reading of a different sort of spy fiction exponent, John Le Carré. My time in the Soviet republics enabled me to understand the machinations and intrigues of Le Carré's dark world of espionage. I was a businessman, not a secret agent, but like Smiley and his colleagues, I always felt I was being watched.

I stated that I was reading Jan Morris' *The Matter of Wales* as I write this memoir. This is significant because it illustrates that I am always attentive to my national and cultural heritage. You might say that you can take the boy out of Bala, but you can't take Bala out of the boy. Morris writes about this heritage: the typical love of words and poetry of the Welsh; the cleverness too, but also the outrageous and often drunken behaviour so often exhibited throughout our Celtic history. These seem to be the building blocks of the edifice we know as Welshness.

Some people think that there is a big difference between North Wales and South Wales, but I have never really felt that there is any animosity between these branches of what is a common tree. I had never played rugby before going to Cardiff to study pharmacy, but I have to say that when I was playing football there my tackling style was somewhat akin to that of a rugby forward. 'They shall not pass' was a personal mantra. Nevertheless, I was quickly accepted by my friends and colleagues, who understood that we are not all built as

155

slinky wingers. More of that word presently.

Most of my college contemporaries were not Welsh speaking, since our native tongue is not all that native to the South Wales coastal belt. I find there is automatically a stronger link if you share a common language, however, and many of my closest friends are bi-lingual. Welsh is my first language, and the language I speak at home. My local GP in Brecon, Arwyn Davies, now retired but a close friend, is a fellow Welsh speaker and I would find it strange indeed if we were to converse in English. Once you start engaging with someone in your native tongue it is almost impossible to switch to another mode of discourse. John Elfed Jones is another man I can only speak to in Welsh. I think any of us would find it almost hurtful if one of us addressed the other in English now.

My current social life involves going out for meals with Ann, sometimes for lunches, sometimes for evening meals, usually at least once or twice a week, sometimes with old friends. I am a little sceptical about meeting new people these days because I enjoy being frank and forthright and do not care much for the idea of having to concentrate on not offending company. It is a blessing denied younger people and a privilege of being older. I heard someone recently describe this attitude as 'purple suit syndrome', in that you feel you could wear a brightly coloured suit if you felt like it, because you no longer have to worry about being answerable to someone for being harmlessly outrageous.

I said that I went to Saundersfoot in the autumn of 2022 for my daughter's birthday. We had a small celebration there but also another party on the Saturday evening in a hostelry back in Brecon, an event attended by some seventy people, mainly friends of Bryony and Hefin. On the Sunday, a large number of these guests congregated at Battle House. The combination of food, alcohol and convivial company was delightful, I must say.

Speaking of food, I would like to offer a word of praise for Chinese cuisine. I do not often indulge in takeaways, because too often I find these are rather thrown together concoctions reliant on a lot of MSG and sugar, but I do go to good Chinese restaurants. When I was in Nigeria I was absolutely spoiled with regard to the best of

Chinese food. There is an interesting contrast with regard to my experience of Chinese meals and my experience of Britain's other national staple, Indian food. Nigeria offered me the most exquisite of Chinese fare and it has rather gone downhill from there. The converse is true of Indian food, because my first encounters with it were in Tiger Bay in a series of Indian restaurants catering for impoverished students. Nowadays I can afford more upmarket versions of Asian delicacies in good restaurants.

A moment ago I was talking about convivial company. Currently I am fortunate in being able to enjoy the company not only of my oldest and closest friends but the company too of younger people, chiefly my daughter's friends. They seem to enjoy coming to Battle House and sometimes they turn up when Bryony is visiting us. She does this fairly regularly. Perhaps the irreverence of my observations about contemporary society is a refreshing contrast to their 'woke' friends' seriousness. Brought up on the absurd humour of *The Goons* and *Monty Python's Flying Circus* as I was, it is possible that people of my age can laugh at and belittle institutionalised folly more readily. I doubt that a comic writer or performer today would come up with a sketch like 'The Ministry of Silly Walks' for fear of offending someone with a disability.

Sometimes I am asked what I think are my greatest achievements and my greatest regrets. Concerning the former, I might be expected to talk about some of my public service roles, such as serving as a governor of the BBC. I am proud of that achievement of course, and proud to be associated in any way with the prodigious talent of many of the people who worked there. Neither would I argue that being chairman of the governing body of Swansea University and chairman of the WDA and The Training and Enterprise Council were anything but substantial testament to my leadership skills.

I would not class my work at the BBC as a professional achievement, however. Probably my greatest achievement in terms of my profession was gaining Qualified Person status as a pharmacist. Under EEC rules, to gain this status you had to demonstrate your judgement in releasing pharmaceuticals onto the market. Just qualifying as a pharmacist was not enough. Most of the Qualified Persons when I began my career were QPs before the registration procedure came in. Accordingly, I was one of the first pharmacists to qualify as a QP in a newer, stricter regime. The process involved oral examination by very experienced pharmacists. An example of what happened was that I was presented with a crab and asked to identify it. 'It's a horseshoe crab,' I responded. Then I was asked what elements this creature might possess which would be of pharmaceutical use. My technique was not to give a simple answer, which would lead to further questions, but spend some time elaborating on my answer. This gave my interlocutors less time to outwit me, as I saw it.

My most truthful answer to the question about my greatest achievement would be to say that it is my success in bringing up my two wonderful children, for it is this that thrills me most. Perhaps I should qualify that. Persuading Ann to marry me was also a masterstroke. This might seem rather pat, but it is true. My determination to provide my children with the very best education was there from the start. Oddly too, for a young man, I was always determined to live in a grand Georgian house. Ann and I agreed early in our life that this was an ambition we both shared, though we did not know where this might be. We were so resolved that we began buying Georgian furniture even while we were still living in a modern house.

It was while I was a student in Cardiff that I was introduced to the idea of living in something more substantial than an ordinary semi-detached home. I had a friend, Chris, whose parents lived in a lovely elegant old house in Cyncoed. When I was invited there, it made me think that such a home, and the concomitant lifestyle, was something I should strive for. I knew it would take considerable wealth to achieve it, inevitably. Some people are spurred on by poverty; I can safely say I was spurred on by wealth, or the prospect of wealth, shall we say.

As to regrets, I wish I had been able to attend a school that would have given me a better opportunity to go to an Oxbridge college for my higher education. I have courted controversy in my professional and public service life, but I do not have any regrets in that regard. I am rather pleased with my own outspokenness and ebullience, as a matter of fact.

One thing I do regret is that I did not continue with my musical education. I had piano lessons from a gifted teacher called Christmas Evans, but as a stubborn eleven-year-old I simply would not practise. I detested Mondays because that was when my weekly lesson took place. Ann was a better student than me, for she passed a number of piano examinations, despite not loving the tedious business of practising either. I also wish I had been able to play rugby. My school was not orientated towards this sport, however. I was therefore too old when I was finally introduced to the game to be any good at it. I have seen through the experiences of friends such as Bryan Shand that one can make a network of influential friends through playing rugby.

I hope my children continue to make a success of their lives. I have great hopes for my grandchildren too. Tomos is currently at St Paul's school in London. It is an excellent school, one of the original nine public schools established by the Clarendon Commission and alma mater of Edmund Clerihew, who invented the four-line poem which bears his name. I trust Tomos will progress to Oxbridge from there. I have no fears about Aneira because she is a powerhouse and will doubtless succeed. Cerys will be fine too, though living in Canada she will suffer from not being in Wales. Perhaps she will return to the land of her fathers. She was, at least, born here.

Wales is a beautiful country but unfortunately I do not believe it has the natural resources to be prosperous. Our only chance is to provide an education for the next generation that is better than anywhere else. I fear the likelihood of this happening is vanishingly small because of the limited vision of our politicians.

I love my homeland and I love my home, but of course I love travel too. One of our best experiences recently was a trip to New Zealand, followed by an excursion to Easter Island, home of the amazing monumental statues, the moai, and thence to Santiago in Chile. I have also been to India, to Shimla, the old headquarters of the Raj. British officials used to migrate to this mountainous region in summer to escape the heat of the Hindustan plains.

I have experienced a safari in South Africa and also spent a little time in Vietnam. We were lucky in that we were able to meet up with Bryony there because she was doing some medical work abroad as part of her studies. I was, of course, fascinated by the history of Vietnam because of the military conflict there, but I also visited Myanmar because of my interest in the Second World War and the phenomenon of the Burma railway. Over 90,000 civilians and about 12.000 British servicemen died in the Japanese army's construction of this link between Bangkok and Rangoon. The film *The Bridge on the River Kwai* documents some of the horrors of this time and it is still a sobering experience to look at what remains of the railway.

I have had less exotic holidays too, naturally. With a young family we were restricted to holidays on mainland Europe. Portugal was a favourite destination, but I also drove to Brittany one year. These days we tend to go to places where we can have guided tours and to places where I can I try to fit in some fishing.

Chapter 13 *Fisherman's Fortune*

I've managed to convince my wife that somewhere in the Bible it says, 'Man cannot have too many shotguns and too many fishing poles.'

Norman Schwarzkopf

My fishing interests are quite revealing, I feel, inasmuch as my father's fascination with the sport was so great that I could not help but be caught up in it. I saw myself very much as his apprentice. I accompanied him whenever I could, and shared lots of his experiences. This plainly brought us closer together. One needs to remember that in the early nineteen fifties fathers were not the figures they are today. They were generally much more remote and tended to leave the business of child rearing to their wives. Of course, they were ready to act as disciplinarians, but often they were not around during their children's waking hours, or sometimes even for at least a part of the weekend. People worked longer hours in those days.

My father, however, had the time to show me and teach me his love of fishing. I should not confess to this perhaps, but I was sometimes persuaded to bunk off school. As I revealed earlier, my father had bunked off work himself, or left early at any rate. I suppose I can be comforted by the thought that it is unlikely any of my old teachers will be reading this memoir. If they are, I apologise, but claim my miscreant behaviour was all in a good cause.

I was very much in my father's shadow. I could not really envisage myself in his shoes. As I say, fathers were heroes to be admired, rather than close allies. This contrasts very much with my attitude to my son and his fishing exploits, I have to say. I took Hefin to some of the best fishing places in the world. Arctic Russia, for instance. This would have been when he was in his late teens. Because of his physique and height, he was a natural fisherman; he has the action to cast out a considerable distance, for instance. I taught him the intricacies and the joys of salmon fishing, whereas my father was not much concerned about me trying to catch the fish. Rather, he was very keen on me helping him. I functioned as his ghillie. I use this term, and not 'servant' because it is the precise Scottish word for the role of faithful retainer on a hunting or fishing trip. It does imply a certain inferiority in status, but it also suggests expertise in the arts of the sports involved.

It is a strange ambition to admit to, but I wanted to be the best ghillie in the world, not the best fisherman. The tasks of the ghillie are to set the rods up, attach the flies, and generally do the preparation work before fishing begins. The morning, or even the whole day, can be lost if flies are tied on faultily and come undone. What you can be certain of is that a ten-pound salmon may not find a weakness, but a thirty- or forty-pound salmon surely will. It is self-evident that we are all in the business of wanting to catch the biggest fish. I have myself caught sea trout weighing over twenty pounds. One of these I have on display in my 'trophy room' – actually a former stable I use as a storeroom. I have caught a bigger fish than that, but that was on a sail fishing expedition off the Pacific coast of Panama, where I caught a two hundred odd pound marlin. That was a struggle!

I should mention that I have done a great variety of different types of fishing. I have fished in the River Dee in my native Denbighshire, but I have also fished in Scotland, Ireland and Norway, and in far flung locations in Russia, Argentina, and even The Falkland Islands. In truth, I will admit I have invested, as I like to think of it, a good chunk of my disposable income on my fishing interests.

My father mainly fished for salmon, but also trout. He knew the rivers extremely well. Aficionados will appreciate that there are differences between types of salmon you will find in different parts of the UK. Dee salmon are long and torpedo shaped; salmon in the River Wye are shaped more like a portmanteau. The nature of the river, its currents and condition, determine the evolution of these differences because some shapes do better than others with regard to their environment. Salmon, of course, always return to their spawning ground and therefore do not change much in evolutionary terms.

Up to the age of ten or eleven, being an expert ghillie was the extent of my fishing ambitions, but, as might be expected, school, an interest in girls, and various other factors intervened. As a result, I did very little fishing during my time in secondary school and my years at university. Living just outside London there was also very little opportunity for fishing either.

Then, when I had set up my own business at the age of thirty or so, I resolved to apply the knowledge I had amassed, or distilled perhaps would be a better term, as apprentice at my father's side. It was a great joy for me now to take my father to some of the best places for us to practise our art. I would not say that my wider experience reversed our roles, with him now my apprentice, because I was aware of the need to be sensitive to his feelings. Instead, we now fished as equals. He had no desire to visit exotic locations like Alaska, but we did go to chalk streams, good for trout fishing, and to private lakes where there were huge trout to be caught, albeit sometimes with a measure of difficulty.

My father was not too bothered by such lakes and ponds, however, preferring to fish in rivers, where he could scrutinise the movement of the water and 'read' the fishes' behaviour. I do recall that at one location, where there was a stipulation that anglers should catch no more than five fish, my father caught five within the first quarter of an hour. I was not as successful, but I was concentrating on trying to reel in a twenty plus pound trout. There is a distinction to be drawn between 'brownies' - I am talking about fish, not paramilitary young girls here - which are smaller, and the more silvery larger trout. When you think about it, catching five trout each weighing five pounds is considerably easier than catching one twenty pounder. The smaller fish tend to swim nearer the surface too, whereas my prey was normally more likely to lurk near the bottom of the lake and be more circumspect about the allure of my fly.

The joy of fishing new rivers was very special. The Ponoi River in the Arctic, for example, teems with Atlantic salmon. It is not the easiest place in the world to get to, however. The river is situated at 67 degrees North and entails a chartered flight to Murmansk, via Helsinki, followed by a two-hour helicopter flight across the tundra to a camp at a place called Ryabaga. There are, of course, no roads in this desolate part of the world. The helicopters are ex-Russian air force, sometimes still with bullet holes in them as evidence of their prior life. There would be a party of international fishermen, many of them Americans, on each trip. And the trips were not inexpensive. I shall share a piece of wisdom here that was common to us all: the secret of good fishing is not to send the invoices home for inspection by your loved ones.

There was invariably a significant camaraderie within the group, despite our different backgrounds. In some ways I was a pioneer for the UK because few British fishermen had undertaken trips to Arctic Russia before. Russia, of course, was still a communist country back then, but the trips were facilitated by the military, who probably took a percentage of the price we had to pay. Though it was difficult for Westerners to gain access to certain parts of the country during this era, politicians tended to turn a blind eye, being largely under the control of the armed forces anyway. Nowadays there is a commercial concern operating the fishing expeditions. Frontiers International Travel arrange trips all across the world. Unfortunately for keen salmon fishermen, however, at the time I am writing this memoir their activity has ceased because of the conflict in Ukraine.

A week's fishing would often cost about five thousand pounds, and this was decades ago, remember. For that you had basic accommodation in one of a number of tents, but we were provided with electricity, shower facilities and excellent food. The organisers did not stint on anything, doubtless bearing in mind the likelihood of repeat custom. The Ponoi does offer the best salmon fishing in the world after all.

I used to go there perhaps twice a year, and I did so for about ten years. The best months are July and September, when there is no ice melt, which makes fishing less pleasant, although the blue colours are extremely attractive.

There are phenomena called the spring run and the autumn run which apply to most Atlantic salmon. In Russia it is different because the rivers are frozen over for a good part of the year. The fish would leave their feeding grounds in Spring but would have to stay in the river over the following winter because they could not break through the ice. They would eventually make their way back to open water the following Spring. You might think that they would starve, because they only feed in salt water, but they manage to survive. They have to live off their own fat reserves, but also there is a huge deficiency between the energy they need and the energy they have, because of their long fasting period.

As I have spoken about before, the movement of the fish's scales as water runs over its body, I believe, provides the creature with the necessary energy for survival. In point of fact, I have spent many waking hours puzzling over this process. Some sleeping hours too, I suspect. What I do know is that life depends on a movement from adenosine diphosphate to adenosine triphosphate. ADP is the premier energy molecule in living cells; ATP acts as a cell's energy storehouse. It enables cells to store energy safely in small packets and release the energy for use only as and when it is needed. In other words, ATP serves to close the gap between energy-releasing reactions like food breakdown and energy-requiring actions like synthesis. I am aware that this explanation may be a tad baffling for some lay people, but perhaps most people would understand the basic principle that animal life depends on such a movement of electrons.

This behaviour of the Ponoi salmon, akin to a sort of suspension of life, does not occur anywhere else in the world. Atlantic salmon live for a number of years, usually about five, so they do not come back to their birthplace to spawn and then die. This is true, however, of their Pacific counterparts. As a scientist, I have always been interested in how we can analyse the scales of a specimen to determine its age. I think it is fascinating that, rather like trees, the scales present with a series of concentric rings which indicate growth stages.

As a side note I should say that I am indebted to my wife Ann for some of my successes in fishing because she encouraged me not to try and use my father's old rods and tackle, but to spend a not inconsiderable amount of money on state-of-the-art gear.

My initial motivation for fishing as a juvenile was partly mercenary, as I have said, because my father and I were able to sell our produce to a range of outlets with some ease. Subsequently, it was much more to do with practising a specific set of skills. I have, of course, eaten some of my catch, and given fish to my friends and family, but my experiences in Arctic Russia, in particular, taught me that it was best to release your catch. There is no real need for an individual to kill fish; trawlermen do enough of that.

I suppose you can say fishing has been a consistent metaphor for my wider life, in that I see it as a manifestation of a very basic human instinct, using the skills you have gained to gain advantage over your adversary. In rivers you outwit the fish; in the boardroom you outwit an equally canny opponent, be it a businessman or a politician. Or even at times a colleague.

For some people the social aspect of the sport is quite important, and as I have just said, I did enjoy the company of fellow anglers in some locations, such as Arctic Russia. We were united in our battle against the elements as well as our prey. I have also derived a good deal of pleasure from fishing with my son, as you might expect. It was slightly different as far as my father was concerned, because we were approaching the activity from different starting points. He was fishing as a sportsman; I was fishing almost as a scientist. This is significant because I think my understanding of the physics and biology of it all enabled me to be more successful than many of my fellow anglers. As I have said a few times already, the potential answers to the question 'Why?' provided me with a series of strategies to gain an advantage over my opponent, as I see it.

In response to critics who might deplore the notion of trophy

166

hunting, I can say that fishing allows you to keep trophies without having to kill your prey. You simply take a photograph of your catch. Of course, it is possible to have a more physical trophy. If you are determined to kill a fish anyway you can freeze it first, put it in a mould and make a cast of it, which you then paint and represent as your trophy. Animal trophies are stuffed taxidermically before being displayed on walls or in glass cases, but the fish you see behind counters in bars are plaster casts or even cleverly carved plaster replicas.

Having had a taste of Arctic Russia, I wanted to fish for the best salmon in other far-flung locations. I have been to rivers in the far Northern reaches of Norway but unfortunately I have never been able to fish in the very best place, the River Alta, because there is a huge waiting list of people waiting for a licence to fish there. You have to wait for a permit holder to give up the sport, which is rare, or to die, in order to move up the long list of hopefuls.

I have fished in Ireland, in The Shannon and in The River Moy, which I preferred. It is a beautiful river that runs through County Sligo and County Mayo on the West coast. and it yields a huge number of salmon every year. Balina, a small town studded with fine Georgian and Victorian four storey houses, was where I stayed on my trips to Ireland.

Fishing in Ireland was very exciting. There was at the time no limit to the number of fish you could catch on the River Moy, so you might find yourself with a haul of twenty or thirty fish after a day's work. Some of these I would bring home and some I would share with other fishermen. John Elfed Jones, whom I have talked about before, was my companion on many of my Irish trips. As chairman of Welsh Water, he had the right connections to arrange things for us. He was a little older than me and in fact had fished with my father, but basically, we have been friends and business associates for much of my life.

In the late nineteen nineties he was commissioned by some venture capitalists to find an up-and-coming company in Wales into which they could invest. I saw this as a great opportunity, and I invited John Elfed to Russia on one of my fishing trips, in order to get to know him better and to find out a little more about the background of these venture capitalists. They had wanted to buy Penn Pharmaceuticals, but nothing came of it. It was a fishing trip in more than one sense, but I did not get a bite, you could say. This took place a couple of years before I did eventually sell the company to my management team.

Emboldened by my Russian fishing experiences I tried other exotic locations. Amongst these were Argentina and The Falkland Islands. There are no salmon in this latter location, but fishing for sea trout can be rewarding too. Landowners, usually sheep farmers, both in Argentina and the Falklands, would take eggs, wrapped in wet moss, and introduce them into the rivers. Once the fish had eaten all the food available to them, they would head on out to sea, where there was an inexhaustible supply of food.

Sea trout are migratory, like salmon, and return to their birthplace to spawn. They are not quite the same adventurers as salmon, however. Salmon migrate all the way up to Greenland, where there is a plentiful supply of krill. They put on weight very quickly and after a year they come back as grilse, about five or six pounds in weight. Sea trout have a rather different diet, since they rely on shellfish caught in river estuaries. They have developed larger, more efficient jaws in order to crush their prey, but this makes catching them much more challenging because their mouths are very hard and therefore resistant to the hook.

It is very windy in Argentina, with water coming down off The Andes. The only similar conditions I have encountered were on the Rio Grande. Readers may be picturing the dusty canyon one sees in John Ford Westerns when I mention this river, but I am talking about the South American river, where the slow-moving water meanders down towards Antarctica.

I fished in Argentina with some fellow Welshmen - hardy souls who had the will (and the financial resources, let it be said) to battle against the elements and our piscine adversary. Ted Turner, of CNN fame and of course also famous as the husband of Jane Fonda, would rent out his estate to us. Sometimes, when I am feeling in a whimsical mood, I tell people I have had the privilege of sleeping in Jane

Fonda's bed, because it is actually true. Ted Turner owned an *estanzia* in Argentina, having bought up sheep stations in order to reintroduce the native guanaco, a type of llama that has evolved to withstand the fiercest weather conditions, into their natural environment. Turner was very big on conservation. He defrayed some of the costs he incurred in this enterprise by charging keen fishermen like me to fish in his territory.

Fishing in the Falkland Islands presented different challenges, insofar as one needed military contacts in order to get on a flight there from the UK. Before the Falklands War it was easy enough, but after the Argentinians had been repelled the authorities were more circumspect. Nevertheless, with Brecon being an important training centre for the army, I was able to use my contacts to get access to transport flights for myself and a couple of colleagues.

The Falkland Islands, I have to say, are not what you would call a fun place, though they did offer good fishing opportunities. There are hotels in Port Stanley which cater for nature tourists and geologists and so forth, so it was reasonably comfortable.

I should mention now a man called Peter Humphries, for he is a significant figure as far as my fishing exploits are concerned. Peter is quite an eccentric chap, and a truly lovely man. A doctor by profession, he was a man of considerable wealth. He had worked in London, but he hails from Cardigan and his GP practice was situated in West Wales. I am not sure how he amassed his wealth, but I suspect some of it must have been family money. He certainly had a lot of influence and was able to gain access to the best fisheries for himself and the circle of friends he fished with. In truth I suspect the actual sport was perhaps of less importance to him than the company of convivial friends on our adventures, which were oftentimes in Scotland.

Peter would gain access for us to select private estates in the highlands. Invariably this entailed making bookings far in advance, more than a year ahead in some cases, because they afforded the very best fishing. We fished the River Tweed and The Spey. The estate ghillie, who knew the water well, would accompany us and advise on what type of fly to use, where to fish on the beat you have chosen, and even where to land the fish, typically on a sandy or gravelly area if you were battling with a large specimen. Of course, having this sort of privilege does not come cheap, and the resources required to fund a salmon fishing trip to one of Scotland's prime locations completely excludes the man in the street.

I can tie flies, but I find it is much easier to buy them. Flies come in different shapes and sizes. If the water is low you tend to use a smaller version. They are not realistic representations of actual flies; they act more as colourful lures which attract by movement and flashes of light. The really important thing is the depth of the fly as it enters the water. You cast out and your lure is carried downstream by the river current. As it passes a salmon's nose, the fish wonders what on earth this phenomenon is. They are not attracted to it as food, of course, since they only feed in salt water, but they are tempted to investigate. Having no opposable thumbs, as it were, they bite into it and hopefully, at least as far as the angler is concerned, they get hooked.

In the estate near Rothes where I often fished, the family would move out for a few weeks and guests would enjoy the resources and hospitality offered by the family's retainers. You might say one was privileged to live the life of a lord for a week or so. Mike Loxton was the main instigator and organiser of trips to this estate. I met him through knowing Peter Humphries. Though they were both medical men it was fishing that brought them together.

Mike Loxton was a remarkable character who lived in Sunningdale, near Windsor. He was a GP, but he only dealt with private patients, who were necessarily pretty affluent people, and often quite important figures in society. As an example of his sphere of influence, he was contacted by authorities in Chile when it was planned to extradite General Pinochet from the UK, after the dictator had been arrested whilst on a visit to London. He was held because there was an international warrant for his arrest on charges of corruption and a whole raft of human rights violations. They used Mike Loxton to mastermind the extradition on health grounds because he was an eminent figure, whose expertise it would have been difficult to challenge. Mike subsequently received an invitation from the Chilean government to fish in Chile, but it has never been established whether this was any form of *ex gratia* payment, of course.

Once you have been accepted by people like Loxton and Humphries into their 'club', it becomes increasingly easy to gain access to the best fishing expeditions. You might get a phone call from one of them asking you if you had a week free in May, say, and you would get to go to Speyside and enjoy the marvellous facilities of some stately home and the joys of salmon fishing at its best. I usually organised my stays on the River Spey through Peter Graham, an estate agent but also responsible for one of the best beats on the river, Delfur, near the town of Rothes. I have also had dealings with Strutt and Parker, the agents responsible for salmon fishery sales on the Spey.

I stated earlier that I once went sailfishing off the coast of Panama, I am not essentially a sea fisherman, but I considered it something I should do once in my life, and Panama seemed an exotic enough location. I had the opportunity to go because of my connections with a group of shooting friends who were organising a trip there.

I am afraid to say that I found the country was not the most salubrious place I have visited, particularly since where we needed to get to in order to fish involved travelling across mangrove swamps to get to the West coast and out into the Pacific Ocean. When you get to the coast there is still a two-hour journey in a twenty-foot boat powered by huge engines to the fishing grounds. It is essentially a young man's game because your bones are shaken to pieces, and you still have the arduous business of trying to catch a fish weighing two or three times your own weight.

On the way out to the areas where you will find marlin you fish for tuna about two feet in length and then you cut them in half to use as bait for the big fish. Then your crew tie you to the mast of the boat, so you are not dragged into the water by the fish's superior strength. When you catch one of these monsters you pull it to the side of the boat and take your trophy photograph. Then you release it. The iridescence of these fish is quite remarkable. The stress they experience does something to their body chemistry and they exhibit a range of blue and purple colours which is quite beautiful.

You would not want to be at sea, or even on a river, in the dark in this part of the world because of the extent of narcotics smuggling that takes place. In films we are used to seeing narcotics being transported in trucks and vans, but Colombian drug barons sometimes find a sea route more expedient in getting their product into the lucrative North American market.

Fishing is much more cerebral than you might suspect. One has to find the right river at the right time of year to be successful. There is very little point in fishing in August, say, when the water is too warm and river levels too low. September is a good month because in the following couple of months the fish will normally be spawning. Accordingly, they get very nervous about everything and refuse to be attracted by a fisherman's lure.

Different species of salmon have different strategies. In the Towy and Cothi rivers, for instance, the big fish will come in during the close season, after mid-October. They will stay for no more than a week then disappear again. Evolution has taught them this strategy.

I also hunt. I shoot pheasant, partridges and duck. I have shot deer in the past too, though deer stalking is surprisingly difficult. Deer are very alert to new sounds and smells in their immediate environment and stalking involves crawling on all fours carrying a rifle, sometimes for a mile or more. It is hard work and requires a level of fitness I no longer boast, sadly. Usually one was hunting a stag, which would be surrounded by a harem of does dedicated to protecting their master. And these does are very skittish. I sometimes think of the stag as analogous to that kind of senior politician who surrounds himself with nervy civil servants to ward off any threat of opprobrium.

I tend to do my shooting in Wales, which has, in my opinion, better shooting than other parts of the country, except in the case of grouse. There are grouse in Wales but, as everyone knows, the finest shooting of this type of game is in the highlands of Scotland. Nevertheless, when a large two and a half thousand acre moor came up for sale near Abergavenny, I bought two of the nine shares that were made available. I entered into partnership with some of my good fishermen friends in this venture, with the belief that I deserved to own a part of some grouse moor, having worked as hard as I had thus far in life.

Now, it is difficult to know what to do with this acreage. It is a fair size and might be attractive to one of the energy companies for them to use for carbon credit purposes. A grouse moor is, of course, ideal as an area which can retain carbon, meaning that an energy company can claim thousands of pounds each year to offset their carbon usage. As I write it has not been sold, however.

The pinnacle of shooting is the grouse. I have had some lovely days on the moor with beaters at Pitlochry, a splendid town just south of the Cairngorms, and on the banks of the Dee. It is, I have to say, a marvellous experience, but also an eye-wateringly expensive one. The way it works is that you are given a fifty-bird day, for example, and you are required to pay for what you shoot. A day's shooting can thus cost seven and a half thousand pounds. And that is the price even if you do not manage to shoot any birds. If you shoot more than your allowance you pay more, typically at a rate of three hundred pounds per brace of grouse. In addition, you have to pay for your food and board for the duration of your stay, though it does tend to be in a fine old castle. I have stayed, for instance, at The Earl of Strathmore's residence, Glamis Castle, as I have already mentioned, though that was on a pheasant shoot rather than a grouse expedition. The castle is very famous for being the childhood home of Her Majesty Queen Elizabeth, the Queen Mother. It is perhaps even more famous, for the literary minded, as the castle where Macbeth and Lady Macbeth killed King Duncan.

Grouse shooting of course commences on the glorious twelfth, August 12th, but I have always thought that that particular day was more suited to its social aspects than strictly the joys of hunting. Some chaps would be in a hurry to get back to their London clubs with their prizes, anticipating a fine grouse dinner with their friends. I was more interested in the sport than such showmanship. The best shooting week is later on, in my view, in September, when the midges, a real nuisance in summer, are less prevalent.

There are two ways in which the grouse can be shot: by deploying a line of beaters, or by a process called 'walking up'. The trouble with this latter method is that it tends to be the younger grouse who are alarmed into flight. When such grouse are killed the age profile of the bird population naturally suffers. Beaters are experienced enough to cause both younger and older birds to take flight and thus a steadier age profile is ensured. Peregrines and hen harriers predate on grouse, but the population remains fairly steady. The red grouse, famous for being the bird on Famous Grouse whisky, for instance, is more in danger through the loss of its habitat than from hunters.

There is also some fine shooting to be had in Wales, for me particularly on an estate called Glanusk, on the way to Crickhowell. You join a syndicate of perhaps eight guns and shoot for about ten days. Again, this is costly. If you have a two hundred bird day, it can cost ten thousand pounds.

I have a good gun, a Churchill, which is probably on a par with the famous Purdey shotgun. It is itself an expensive piece of ordnance. I have seen second-hand examples selling for £10,000. It has a shorter barrel than most guns, twenty-five inches, which allows a shooter to raise his gun more quickly than is the case with a longer barrelled weapon. The makers, E. J. Churchill, reasoned that range was less important than speed of reaction in the sport. I am self-taught, but it is perhaps not as difficult as it might seem. With a rifle you have a single bullet, but a shotgun cartridge expels a sphere of pellets into which the bird will fly, depending on what type of gun you are using. A longer barrelled gun may create more of a tubular spray of pellets; a Churchill gun a more spherical spray. It all depends on the type of pellets you use, and you have to take into account wind conditions too, plainly. In many ways what I enjoy is the science of the sport, not simply the fact of outwitting the bird, or providing food for the table.

Chapter 14 *Reflections*

I like fishing when I don't catch anything as much as when I do
Matt Lauer

I began this memoir by saying that nothing much of great import occurred on the day of my birth, 2nd July 1943. It is not quite true. Detroit Red Wings defeated Boston Bruins (4-0) to win the Stanley Cup. I have to say, that means nothing to me, but something else also occurred which I think does have a certain resonance and relevance, if only as a metaphor.

It was on this day, I believe, that the Slinky was invented. The Slinky, for anyone unfortunate enough never to have been presented with one as a child, is a toy that was developed by an American naval engineer, Richard T. James, in Philadelphia. It is basically a springy coil of steel wire manufactured with precision to create the precise tension required for it to do what it does, namely right itself if it falls over. In addition to its use as a toy, it has been used as a classroom teaching tool and as a portable and extendable radio antenna in wartime (particularly the Vietnam War). But it was by accident that it was invented.

James was trying to develop springs that could support and stabilise sensitive instruments aboard ship in rough seas when he accidentally knocked one of the springs off a shelf. He watched as the spring 'stepped' in a series of arcs to a stack of books, to a tabletop, and to the floor, where it re-coiled itself and stood upright. It was fascinating to watch and gave him the idea to market the spring as a toy.

Why am I saying this? The name Slinky was decided upon as a term which suggested notions of sleekness and grace. I am not sure if those terms are totally accurate descriptions of me. But the ability to stumble and correct myself and assume my position again without seeming effort definitely applies to my working life, I would like to think. I have, as any successful businessman must have, the facility to re-form when occasion demands. Whether this comes from circumstance or character is moot, of course. I try to tell myself that it is self-belief that has prompted me to the successes I have managed to achieve. Some might call it arrogance rather than confidence. The term is a tad brutal but perhaps I cannot entirely refute the charge. Whatever, I have stepped from pharmacist to marketer to businessman to researcher and thence to manager, consultant and public service leader with the assiduous and incorrigible skills of my twin the Slinky. I have tried to do so with grace too. As for sleekness? Hmmm.

I would like to conclude with another quotation from William Bruce Cameron, who said with perhaps undue modesty: 'I've always been busy, but I wasn't always successful.' It is definitely true that I have always been busy. To this day, in my eightieth year, I retain interests in a number of projects, including the time-consuming but gratifying task of writing this memoir, of course. I confess that I was not always successful either, but I am proud of many of the things I have done. And, above all, I have enjoyed the challenges and the duels I have faced, and the partnerships and the alliances I have formed with some wonderful people in both my professional and personal life.

My immense gratitude to you all.

www.ingramcontent.com/pod-product-compliance
Lightning Source LLC
Chambersburg PA
CBHW060648150426
42813CB00052B/464